Just Sharing

JUST SHARING

*A Christian Approach to the
Distribution of Wealth,
Income and Benefits*

Edited by
Duncan B. Forrester
and Danus Skene

EPWORTH PRESS

British Library Cataloguing in Publication Data

Just sharing: a Christian approach to the
distribution of wealth, income and benefits.
1. Wealth – Christian viewpoints
I. Forrester, Duncan B.   II. Skene, Danus
261.8'34

ISBN 0–7162–0443–6

First published 1988
by Epworth Press
Room 195, 1 Central Buildings,
Westminster, London SW1H 9NR

Printed in Great Britain by
Billings & Sons Ltd
Worcester

CONTENTS

MEMBERS OF THE WORKING PARTY

Russell Barr, Minister of Garthamlock, Glasgow

Kay Carmichael, Hon. Fellow, Department of Christian Ethics, University of Edinburgh

Claus Clausen, Community Minister in Hamilton.

David Donnison, Professor of Town and Regional Planning, University of Glasgow, formerly Chairman of the Supplementary Benefits Commission

Timothy Duffy, Roman Catholic Justice and Peace Commission

Duncan Forrester, Professor of Christian Ethics, University of Edinburgh (Convener)

Anne Miller, Lecturer in Economics, Heriot-Watt University, Edinburgh

Simon Robinson, Anglican Chaplain to Heriot-Watt University, Edinburgh

Danus Skene, School Teacher, Forres

John Sleeman, Lecturer in Economics, University of Glasgow

Fred Twine, Lecturer in Sociology, University of Aberdeen

Chris Wigglesworth, General Secretary, Church of Scotland Board for World Mission and Unity, formerly Lecturer in Practical Theology, University of Aberdeen

George Wilkie, formerly Minister of Viewforth Parish Church, Kirkcaldy, and Industrial Mission Organiser for the Church of Scotland

INTRODUCTION

The study of which this book is the fruit is based on the conviction that the sharing of material things and justice in distribution are profoundly spiritual matters. Some might remind us that Jesus refused to adjudicate on the division of an inheritance: 'Who made me a judge or divider over you?' He then proceeded to warn against covetousness, 'for a man's life does not consist in the abundance of his possessions'. The parable of the rich fool who put his trust in his possessions follows (Luke 12.13–21). But this narrative in fact reminds us that our task, the true function of theology, is to probe below the surface of contemporary problems. A person is more than possessions, or lack of them. Covetousness, mammon worship – or to give them a modern title, 'possessive individualism' – are perennial dangers which corrode community and spiritual values. 'Heaven on earth' is far other than an increase in material prosperity for the majority of the population, while others are deprived, powerless and poverty stricken. It has to do with justice and fellowship with God and our fellows.

This emphasis on distribution as a spiritual matter is in continuity with a significant strain in the Christian tradition, which has been stressed strongly in Scotland. Our study seeks to stand within that heritage. In the early nineteenth century, Thomas Chalmers attempted to restore what he called 'godly commonwealth' in Scotland, in which the whole community was to meet the needs of its weak and needy members. And in the Scottish Reformation there was a particularly strong stress on God's call for justice for the poor and oppressed. This concern should be shared by all Christians because it springs directly from the Gospel and from the Christ who came to preach good news to the poor and to announce the acceptable year of the Lord. But the church has not always been faithful to this insight. Professor Smout's fine book, *A Century of the Scottish People 1830–1950* (Collins 1986), is a searing account of poverty, human degradation and social division in nineteenth- and early twentieth- century Scotland as a result of appalling maldistribution. It also shows that the churches failed almost entirely to recognize these things as the great issues for the Christian conscience, said little that could be regarded as prophetic, and failed to challenge injustice and oppression. We should be faithful to the earlier, and more authentic tradition.

The General Assembly of the Church of Scotland at its meeting in 1984, 'recognising the fundamental importance of a system of distribution of wealth, income and benefits which incorporates Christian values', called for the initiation of this study. Accordingly the Church and Nation Committee established a working party on distribution issues which was convened by the Reverend Professor Duncan Forrester of Edinburgh and composed of people with a wide range of expertise and experience. The working party met regularly over a two-year period and received information, advice and opinions from a wide variety of sources. A brief report on the working party's work and conclusions was received and debated by the General Assembly in 1987, and congregations and Kirk Sessions were encouraged to discuss these matters further. We now present the fuller version of our report which we hope will enable wide and informed debate on these issues in the churches and in other circles. Although we give some special attention to the situation in Scotland and in the Church of Scotland, we believe that the questions we raise are of importance for all Christians, and indeed for everyone who cares about the future of our society.

We were glad that our remit concerned distribution, the whole way in which things are shared in our society. This discouraged us from looking at poverty as a problem *out there*, an accidental defect in an otherwise healthy society, something that prosperous Scotland can solve from its surplus without any real disturbance. We, the prosperous and powerful, are part of the problem. So is the church. This must be recognized before we can move towards a solution. The problem is how our society distributes its resources. And a society that tolerates or neglects increasing poverty is a sick society.

Our first task was to *face the facts*, and discover something of what these facts mean in human terms for individuals, for families, for the nation. We learned that if you take the supplementary benefit level as an officially recognized standard of poverty, in February 1985 18.7% of the Scottish people were living in poverty, and another 12.9% were on the margins of poverty. We saw how poverty is concentrated geographically in ghettos of deprivation, and socially among the long-term unemployed, families with young children, the aged, and the unemployed. While the majority prosper, the poor are trapped in poverty. We understood that poverty is not simply about shortage of money. It is about exclusion and power, about relationships and loss of self-respect, it is about lack of choice and limitation of freedom. But all these things are related to lack of money.

We then moved on to *reflection and interpretation*, looking to the Bible and the Christian tradition for clues, insights, signals and challenges. For the facts made us variously angry, frightened or threatened. Our own interests and possessions are involved – and this makes it particularly difficult to bring every thought and prejudice and attitude into captivity to Christ. But this is what Christians must attempt if they are to make any distinctive contribution.

We found in the tradition that possessions and the way they are used are symbols and expressions of love and justice, or of idolatry and selfishness. Community demands the sharing of material, as of spiritual, things. Christianity has deep, rich and sometimes disturbing insights into fellowship.

Thirdly, we went on to discuss how we should *respond* to what we had found – in other words, how do we respond to

Jesus Christ and the neighbours he has given us in today's Britain? The only credible response we felt must be on three fronts simultaneously:

Our personal life-style – how do we deal with our possessions and open ourselves to the need, and the people, around us?

The life of the church – how may each congregation be an experiment in community and in sharing? How may the whole church provide a foretaste of the just sharing and fellowship of the Kingdom of God?

Public policy – this is contentious ground, but we cannot responsibly as Christians and as citizens in a democracy refuse to enter it. We need to help people to rise above a sense of fatalism and impotence. There *are* things we can do, and there are choices we can make. We have indicated in the final chapter some of the options to which we feel priority should be given.

Our working party brought together a fascinating range of experience and expertise. But none of us is poor. We all have a security which means that we have never experienced from the inside the powerlessness and vulnerability of the poor, what deprivation and exclusion mean today. We have not had our children going hungry to bed, been unable to make ends meet, or felt politically impotent. But we listened to the poor. And a woman in Easterhouse, after describing what poverty means for her, reminded us: 'The church should be teaching people about God. So everything's its business.' And that means it is our concern, and yours.

All the members of the working party wrote drafts and working papers which, after discussion by the group as a whole, have contributed to this book. We were surprised and pleased as the project drew towards a close to discover how broad was our agreement. Not every member of the working party would personally endorse every detail of this book. And much interesting and important material the group produced has had to be left out. But several of our working papers, giving data and arguments more fully than was considered appropriate here, are to be separately published and will be available from The Centre for Theology and Public Issues, New College, The Mound, Edinburgh.

We want to thank the many people who spoke with us and made suggestions to help in our work. A number of people made expert, detailed and constructive comments on our drafts. We are particularly indebted in this connection to Mr Wreford Voge of Ernst and Whinney, Dr David Heald of Glasgow University, Professor Adrian Sinfield of Edinburgh University, and Dr Charles Elliott, the former Director of Christian Aid. Miss Chris Brown MBE and Miss Norma Reynolds provided splendid secretarial backup. We are grateful to them all.

To avoid repetition, references have been done in the following way: in the text, author, date of publication, and relevant page number are given in brackets after the quotation; at the end of the book, under *References*, the books cited are listed alphabetically by author.

Chapter One

DISTRIBUTION EXPERIENCED

The way things are distributed affects people, and it affects
fellowship. It is not enough to say that distribution is an
economic problem, or to present the facts and statistics. Any
pattern of distribution not only expresses but confirms
attitudes to human beings and to society, assumptions about
the worth of human beings and the kind of community that
we ought to live in. So distribution raises fundamental issues
of values, of theology, and of attitudes to life. We will discuss
these matters in due course.

People have feelings about distribution. Recognized injustice in distribution makes people angry or bitter. Poverty
involves a major reduction in life chances, and poor people
tend to be marginalized or excluded from the community.
Rich people, on the other hand, according to the gospel,
have great difficulty in entering the Kingdom of God. Many
Christians are deeply concerned that increasing gulfs between
the rich and the poor in our society are profoundly immoral
and destructive. Prosperous people are prone to believe that
their prosperity is the fruit of their hard work – and that
others are poor because they are idle and feckless. But it is
not as simple as that. And even if it were, Christians believe
we are instructed to love our neighbours and help them in
their need.

In Britain today the majority of people, the people in work,
are on the whole quite prosperous. A very small number are
earning colossal salaries. A minority, but an increasing minority, lives in poverty. Many people in prosperous Britain
do not believe that there is significant poverty left in our

country. Much of it is invisible. There is a great deal of
ignorance about how other people live and, above all, what it
feels like to be on the dole, or on supplementary benefit,
about what long-term unemployment does to family life.

In this first chapter we are attempting to do two things.
First, some of the members and consultants of the working party give their 'testimony' about how they have been
affected by encountering profoundly unfair patterns of distribution. David Donnison, a senior academic who has been
Chairman of the Supplementary Benefits Commission and of
the Public Schools Commission, meditates on experiences
which have led him to affirm a connection between a more
equal form of distribution and healthy community life, with
respect for individuality. Chris Wigglesworth, a Church of
Scotland minister who worked in the slums of Bombay and
in development and famine relief projects in rural India and
in Africa, describes how this has shaped his understanding
of the church and of his own vocation. Russell Barr, a young
minister whose first charge is in a Scottish Urban Priority
Area, has been led to rethink his theology and his understanding of the Christian faith through what he has learnt
from the people of Easterhouse.

The second section of the chapter consists of case studies.
They are all authentic, although names and some other details
have been altered to preserve anonymity. One case comes
from Bombay; the rest are Scottish. And the cases are enhanced by extracts from a discussion which we had with a
group of women in Easterhouse.

A. Testimony

1   Comradeship and community: David Donnison

Egalitarians are often accused of indulging in 'the politics of
envy', and this tempts them to reply that they, too, deplore
an envious world, and – unlike their critics – they are prepared to remove the massive and indefensible inequalities
which are the cause of that envy: a justifiable debater's riposte,
but too superficial to start anyone thinking afresh.

Seeking to create a more equal world does not *feel* like envy. It does not even feel as if money and material wealth were the central issues. So what *is* it about? It is about creating a world in which people find it easier to see and hear each other, not treating each other as objects; a world in which it is easier to treat other people with respect and kindness, even when we disagree profoundly with them; a world, if you like, in which it is easier to be good and harder to be bad. But where does equality come in?

The world we actually live in so often seems almost to compel us to treat other people in, at best, a guarded fashion, and at worst with suspicion or outright hostility. Our critics regard those as permanent features of a race filled with original sin, living under governments powerless to make any significant impact on society. The wise man accepts that this is the world he must live in and, imbibing its poisons, acquires what immunity he can.

> The thoughts of others
> Were light and fleeting,
> Of lovers' meeting
> Or luck or fame.
>
> Mine were of trouble,
> And mine were steady,
> So I was ready
> When trouble came.

– as A. E. Houseman said. Yet all are not compelled to swallow the poison or to dish it out. We are all lucky enough to know people who seem to surmount those sad and crippling pressures. By luck, love or hard labour, people do change the worlds they live in, both for the better and for the worse.

When I first joined the navy I spent time in barracks and transit camps where men flowed through, coming off ships for a few days or weeks before being drafted out to sea again. And it was an awful world. No one gave anyone anything: not even information. I lost right away the nice hair brush my mother had given me, and quickly learnt that we could not turn our backs upon our few possessions for one moment without losing them. Later I served in a destroyer, a mine-sweeper and other ships, and was moved by the kindness and comradeship of their crews. Your possessions were safe. People took care of each other. A man who came aboard drunk when the ship was in port would be told to turn in, and the fellow he was about to relieve would stand his watch for him – thereby working for twelve or sixteen hours at a stretch – rather than expose the ship to danger or his drunken comrade to punishment. And whether he liked the man or not played no part whatsoever in that comradely act. Then I went back to a transit camp on my way to another posting, and it was as awful as before. Yet, in a ship or a barracks, these were the same men.

Take another example from years later. As chairman of the Public Schools Commission, then studying secondary schools of every kind in an attempt to prepare workable plans for the grant-aided and independent day schools, I led a group of Commissioners to take evidence in Edinburgh. That city had the most elaborately stratified education system we had found anywhere in Britain: independent boarding schools, independent day schools, grant-aided schools, fee-paying selective state schools, free selective schools, comprehensive schools, secondary modern schools . . . all competing with each other. Meanwhile – to complicate things still further – parents struggled to buy or rent houses in neighbourhoods served by the best schools of each type.

A group of parents (The Edinburgh and Midlothian Association for the Advancement of State Education) came before us to give evidence which I shall never forget. Their message was simple: 'For the sake of our children', these mainly middle class people said, 'we are compelled to compete to get them into the best schools available, knowing that those at the bottom of the pecking order have had so many of the talented pupils and teachers creamed out of them. We hope your recommendations will help to create a comprehensive system in which every school will give its pupils the opportunities we want for our own children. Then we shall no longer have to choose between being good citizens and good parents.'

We have all had similar experiences. Richard Titmuss's book, *The Gift Relationship*, gives a particularly telling example, describing the way in which blood donors have created a nationwide service, providing blood for unknown fellow citizens without asking for payment – whereas in other countries, where the health services work on more mercenary principles, blood donors too demand payment, and the risks of lethal infection from people who have nothing left to sell but their blood are much greater. The whole society is thereby morally impoverished.

Every act – and certainly every act of governments – makes it a little easier or a little harder for all of us to treat each other as comrades: not as objects, but as people whom we really see and hear; people whom we respond to with respect, trust and kindness, whether we like them or not. Amongst comrades, differences in power, status and wealth – modest differences – can be cheerfully accepted without envy, if they are earned in some way by talent and hard work, by the happiness their possessors give the rest of us, or the responsibilities they bear on our behalf. Gross or inexplicable differences in power, status and wealth are not accepted – even for themselves – by people who value comradeship. They would destroy something which is more important.

Building that kind of world is very difficult. It takes generations to make much progress, and all that has been gained can be thrown away again very quickly. In creating a world which makes it a little easier to be good and a little harder to be bad, people are developing and refashioning their own moral standards. For better or for worse, they are constantly making new ways of life possible. They are creating the human race as they go along. It is a mistake to call them 'human beings': they are 'human *becomings*'.

That, rather than envy, is what the pursuit of greater equality is about.

2   *Maldistribution encountered: Chris Wigglesworth*

There is an irony in trying to write about the wrong distribution of the world's goods, sat at a word processor, and
with half my mind thinking about how much my wife and I
can afford to borrow for a house. It is tempting to drop the
attempt to do either or both in a feeling of guilt and annoy-
ance but once you have experienced Indian poverty and an
African drought at first hand, the images never leave you
and my heart aches again when the TV brings the latest ones
into the room – tonight it is Mozambique . . .

The images are as sharp as the first time I saw them:
August 1974 – a bundle of dirty grey cotton under a gleaming
marble pillar in Bombay's VT railway station, which revealed
the wizened and anxious face of an elderly Maratha farm-
labourer, surprised and relieved that someone would listen
as he told how he had lain there for a couple of days, separated from the younger members of the family when they had
travelled without tickets into the big city, away from the
hopelessness of a village where there was no work and little
food into a frightening city with no friends and still no
food . . .

It brings to mind a village scene: Wahegaon, Maharashtra,
India 1971: hot and dry with a grey-brown dust that stings
the eyes and nostrils, cracked dry mud house walls and a
still, silent huddle of men, young and old, sitting and waiting:
'We have no food in the village, the government promised
scarcity grain but there is none, we will wait and see
what happens' – and my feeling of angry helplessness because this village was the next one beyond where our famine
relief supplies could be stretched – used as 'food for
work', supplies provided to pay for manual labour building
a 'murrum' (broken rock and sub-soil) road. We were involving about ten thousand men and women in building roads
between some fifteen villages and as the drought struck
deeper we got deputations from neighbouring villages quietly
asking if they could work for a food ration too. The feeling of
'at least we are doing something' and the impressive sight of
two thousand people at a time building a stretch of new road

with quiet determination had given way to realizing the scale of hunger and need. The few words used and the expression in elders' eyes as they accepted the fact that we could do nothing for their people shattered any feeling of self-satisfaction, but it left the conviction that such things should not and need not happen. It was not easy to eat at nights after days of living in a famine: it is as though the dust gets into your soul. And every further experience becomes harder to write about, other than in the clinical, objective terms needed for reports and plans for projects to be implemented, or for generalized discussions of 'the problems of poverty'.

The term 'maldistribution' is missing from many dictionaries but the reality itself is impossible to evade if you are one of the very large number of people who experience it in the form of thirst, or hunger, or bad housing, or lack of income. Underlying these, and all the other evidence of the highly unequal and unfair way in which wealth, income and benefits are actually shared out, is that sense of powerlessness to change things and even the feeling that there is no point in telling other people. It is a recognition of this lack of power and hope among those who can be called the victims of maldistribution which has to be at the heart of any adequate Christian understanding of poverty. And with it should be an awareness of the tremendous resources within 'the poor' to struggle against heavy odds, to achieve impressive results when not prevented, let alone encouraged, and often to give us profound insights into what life is all about.

It is hardly surprising, on the other hand, that those who do have the power to obtain what they want to drink, and those who wonder how much they ought to eat of what they can easily afford but do not need, and those whose income allows them to select the one or more houses they want to live in, are strangely unaware of the defective nature of distribution. More often than not, the beneficiaries of our patterns of distribution are inclined to believe that things are by and large fairly well apportioned 'by market forces', at least in our country if not in the 'Third World'. Those of us with a reasonable income are prone to believe that too much

of it is 'taken away' in tax, and that any minor redistribution
which may be needed is best done through personal gifts to
'reliable charities'. Even for those with the interest and
opportunity to read this report, it probably requires a delib-
erate effort to find out what it is really like for the 'worse-
off'. It can be a disturbing experience . . .

Another image: late at night, driving a Land Rover loaded
with water supply equipment from Safawa refugee camp, in
the middle of nowhere on the Sudan/Ethiopia border, on a
wretched track with the dust of the drought turning to mud
as the rains finally came, to Wad Kowli camp ('the nearest
thing to hell on earth': BBC, some day in May 1985) and in
the dark passing more than fifteen hundred men, women
and children, silently walking back into Ethiopia, their few
belongings, some food supplies and their surviving babies on
their backs, determined to go home and plant crops now the
rains had come, with little idea whether they would make the
week or two's trek or not. And a few hours earlier I recall
listening to a young nurse talking through her feelings about
leaving babies to die because there were not enough saline
drips for the severely malnourished children all to get one,
deciding which little ones might be most likely to benefit . . .

For me, unfair distribution has been made all too real by
such experiences, by working with and getting to know some
of its victims in very different parts of the world. Amongst
them have been landless labourers in several states across
India and that Sudan-Ethiopia border in Africa. All over
the so-called Third World you will meet men, women and
children who have been forced to abandon their small village
huts and go away. Drought or flooding or some other disaster
have again and again meant that in those rural areas where
most of the world's people live there is little or no water or
food or work, unless you are rich. As a result, each day
thousands of them straggle into the cities, hoping to find
a space in crowded shanty-towns or alongside the railway
lines, with too many of their children living on the broken-up
pavements, like the young man described in a case-study

below (p. 22–4). In other places they walk for weeks, seeing some of their old folk and babies die on the journey, until they reach a crowded refugee camp distributing water and food.

Such are the dramatic cases which attract the belated concern of the West. Yet it is even more significant that in these and many other less well-publicized places it is not only when a specific disaster strikes that food is lacking for those with little purchasing power, who very often are the ones who work to grow and harvest that food. It is normal today in many Third World rural areas for those with little land to have to mortgage it to get out of debt, forcing them to join the ranks of the landless who increasingly swell the cities in search of food and work. There they join the ragged army of cheap labour which keeps wage rates down and working hours long; with many more at subsistence level, including so many children whose only schooling is learning to collect litter to be sold as waste paper and where to find left-over food from the wedding receptions of the wealthy for their daily meal.

Whatever the satisfaction that might be gained by being able to provide some help, usually to small groups of people in such situations, sooner or later one is forced to ask about the causes and the possibility of lasting answers, as opposed to short-term solutions. Such questioning is made more urgent by meeting wealthy people in beautiful homes, sometimes within a minute or two's walk from an urban hutment, or a few miles' jeep-ride from a grim relief-camp, who mostly feel there is nothing they could or should do about changing things. Not to mention the well-meaning upper-class Christians here who keep telling me that what these people need is the gospel. But, I tell them, many of these folk are Christians anyway and may be it is you who need really to hear the gospel call to repent and believe . . .

So that may be why once one has experienced such obscenely unequal distribution, there comes a greater sensitivity to the existence of a parallel division of wealth and power within Britain. What David Sheppard has termed 'The

Other Britain' becomes much more visible once one begins to question the way things are. I found no incongruity in coming back from Sudan and somehow becoming a Regional Councillor for a ward with too many badly-housed people in it. Many try to play off the poor and powerless of the Third World against the 'relatively deprived' here: 'Of course you've seen real poverty, people here should be grateful for the Welfare State' usually seems to be said by people with private health insurance, over £15,000 a year, a car and their own house.

Maldistribution shows here in such things as the difference of house size between, for example, prosperous suburban detached villas and inner-city tenement flats; with a corresponding difference in educational and subsequent employment opportunities for the children living in them. Only a few months of getting to know people in one or two of the euphemistically termed 'difficult-to-let' housing schemes is sufficient to share some experience of lives so lacking in opportunity for change for the better as to be every bit as unacceptable as those of many people in any Indian hutment. Equally striking is the widespread reluctance amongst suburban residents, not to mention church congregations, to recognize the extent of a whole range of distributional inequalities within their own city, let alone Britain as a whole. The evidence is here too of the same potential in communities of 'the deprived' to contribute a lot to curing the ills, not only of their own lives but also of the wider society, if we care to listen.

3   'Who's laughing now?': Russell Barr

'People would laugh at me if I told them but I am sure you know how hard it was for people like myself to live on a low income.'

I had taken Elizabeth's wedding service in the autumn of 1986. She had been a member of our congregation for a number of years, and she had been involved in many of its groups and activities. Her wedding day had been a great occasion, and now she was writing to let me know how she was coping with married life.

The story was familiar. Although she and her new husband were very happy together, Elizabeth wrote of how it
was taking time for her to settle into a new part of the
country, a new home, a new life. There was, however, one
very important change in her lifestyle: her new husband had
found a job.

'One thing I do enjoy is I can now afford to have lunch
every day, not just the main meal in the evening.'

Since July of 1979 I have been the Church of Scotland's
minister in the Parish of Garthamlock and Craigend East,
local authority housing schemes in the north-east of Glasgow,
part of greater Easterhouse. Such a place did not provide
my own home background. My conventionally middle-class
background, with attitudes shaped accordingly, brought me
to university in 1972 with only the vaguest of notions that I
might become a minister of the church.

Things changed when I came in touch with Edinburgh
divinity students who, as the Missionary Society, were en-
gaged in practical projects in areas of deprivation. One of
these, in association with Tom Gordon, then minister of the
Old Kirk in Pilton, involved taking a number of the children
from his parish for a week's holiday during the summer. The
experience of visiting the family homes of these children
changed my life. Here were squalor and deprivation and
housing conditions that I never knew existed – and all but a
short distance from Princes Street, one of the great tourist
attractions of Western Europe. I had been hit by the prover-
bial ton of bricks. In due course, after graduation and marriage,
I was called to the Parish of Garthamlock and Craigend East.
Easterhouse, of which my parish is a part, has the reputation
of being a blight on the face of Scotland. Built in the early
1950s along with other 'schemes' such as Castlemilk and
Drumchapel, Easterhouse takes its name from a village in the
area. There is no longer any such village. Easterhouse is now
the umbrella name given to a number of schemes of which
Garthamlock and Craigend are two.

In a Strathclyde University paper the authors remind us

that Easterhouse was originally created as a solution, not a problem:

> Unlike many urban crisis points elsewhere in Britain and abroad, Easterhouse is not the relic of the industrial revolution or the unplanned development of the nineteenth century, but a modern housing estate conceived and developed as part of the answer to urban decay and dereliction in central Glasgow (Keeting and Mitchell, 1986).

The complex story of how the 'solution' became itself a 'problem' has yet to be fully told. With all the wisdom of hindsight, it still seems extraordinary that the original development omitted such basic amenities as shops. It was only in 1972, nearly twenty years after the first people moved into the area, that the Easterhouse Township Shopping Complex was opened. In my own parish the community had to wait until the early 1980s for the first public hall to be opened. In terms of accepted criteria for housing, health, employment, education and the like, my parish bears all the hallmarks, and scars, of an area of multiple deprivation.

The church has been present in the community from the day the first residents moved into their new homes. The present worshipping congregation of about 175 people comprises two distinct groups. There remain a small and dwindling number of the original residents who tell of a golden age, when one garden was nicer than the next, and when there was a waiting list of people who wanted to live there. The second and larger group consists of more recent residents who are as new to the church as they are to the area.

Facts and figures about a place like Garthamlock and Craigend are one thing, but is harder to speak of the people, of what it is like to live in an area of multiple deprivation. The popular image is one of violence, and while it is true that life in Easterhouse has its violent moments, that is not the dominant reality. For thousands upon thousands of people it is the place where they try to live out the normal routine of life.

If I were to use one word to sum up what it is like to live

in Easterhouse, that word would have to be 'despair'. The despair is tangible. It can be tasted. A little differently, one of our elders speaks of the appalling 'greyness' of the people. Much of the joy and colour of life has been knocked out of them.

That a model of ministry emerged for me was due in no small measure to John Cook, for fifteen years minister in St George's and St Peter's, also in Easterhouse. He told me how in his early days in the area his heart used to be in his mouth as he went to knock on some of the doors and visit people around his parish. He shared his fear with a social worker who was himself a Christian, and got a scolding for being afraid. Did he really think that he, John Cook, would be taking God into that home? Surely he had enough faith to realize that God was already there and if that was so, what was there for him to fear.

It always seems to take someone else to see the obvious. The insight was invaluable for me. Did I think that it was my task to take God to the people of Garthamlock and Craigend? What arrogance! God was already there. Many people already knew his presence and had been trying to live out their Christian faith long before I ever appeared on the scene.

With my own background, I could never fully identify with my parishioners, or they with me. But I could participate in their life, trying to walk a bit of the road with them, making links between their life experiences and the Kingdom of God as I understood it. In the end I would leave, literally and metaphorically, for each person must make their own response to Jesus' invitation to follow him.

In our attempt to be the people of God in Easterhouse we have found it useful to focus our attention on something Jesus once said when questioned by the Jewish Pharisees about the commandments.

Jesus answered, Love the Lord your God with all your heart, with all your soul and with all your mind. This is the greatest and most important commandment. The second

most important commandment is like it, love your neighbour as you love yourself (Matt. 22.37).

It has seemed to us that Jesus is calling us to worship and to
service.

Love the Lord your God ...   It has been a joy for many people
living in Garthamlock and Craigend to worship God, who
welcomes them lovingly into his family. This is of great
importance in a community where so much of life leaves
people feeling themselves to be second-class citizens. The
understanding of family, of belonging to the family of God
whether or not you have a job, whether you are a single
parent, whether you have money to put in the plate or a coat
to put on your back, is an important theme in our worship.
We have even learned that it is important to be able to be
angry with God and before God.

Love your neighbour ...   Just as our life in the community
informs our worship, so does our worship lead us to bear
witness to our faith in the community in which we live. I
want to mention two ways in which that sharing of our
Christian faith in the life of the community has worked itself
out in practice.

Unemployed Workers Centre   In the absence of official figures
for the area it is generally agreed that the unemployment rate
in the Garthamlock area is about 70%. In 1980 our Kirk
Session made a response to this grim situation: a recreation
and resource/information club was started in the church halls.
After a couple of flourishing years it became clear that there
was the need for a separate centre. After negotiation, funds
were secured and a Centre for Unemployed Workers was
built adjacent to the church. The Centre runs independently
with its own staff.

Elderly Care Project   During 1984, concern had been gather-
ing about the needs and conditions of many of the elderly
and housebound in our parish area. While it was clear that
many of them had particular needs requiring attention,

it was also clear that the various statutory and voluntary organizations geared to meeting these needs did not know that at 41 Porchester Street resided Mrs A . . . who could do with their help and Mrs A . . . certainly did not know how to bring her need to their attention. We sought to provide a bridge. Under the auspices of the Manpower Services Commission our Kirk Session sponsored a Community Programme employing six people. Their task was to identify where the elderly and housebound of the parish lived and by means of a short interview establish whether or not they had any particular needs. If anything was discovered, then the appropriate agency would be informed and the matter followed through to its conclusion. At the time of writing, the Project has been awarded funding for a third year and it is no exaggeration to claim that in small ways, and in large, the quality of life of hundreds of people has been improved by the work undertaken.

Being so closely involved I find it difficult to see what the future holds for the parish. It has changed since 1979. There are improved resources, with an Adult Education Centre, a Playbarn, and a Family Centre, in addition to the projects I have mentioned. The active Community Council in Craigend has refurbished two school huts into a Community Centre.

The housing stock has changed. In 1980, some 400 homes were knocked down in the Garthamlock area, the ground being allowed to lie derelict. In 1985, an area of land on the north side of the scheme was leased by the District Council to a private firm, and by the end of 1986 some fifty homes had been built and sold with more being planned. It is as yet much too early to say what effects these changes will have on the community as a whole.

The economic base of the community has continued to decline. Poverty has undoubtedly increased. It is hard to be optimistic. I fear we will reap a bitter harvest from the frustrations of young people who leave school with neither job nor opportunity.

I have come to share the anger and resentment of those

who live in poverty while huge pay increases are given to some already well-paid members of our society.

But my final word is one of gratitude to people like Elizabeth with whose letter I began. For eight years I have shared with her and many like her a little of their struggle to retain human dignity and self-respect. It has been a moving and enriching experience. You see, there was once a time in my life when I might well have laughed on hearing Elizabeth's story. Thankfully, not any more.

B. Cases

What does poverty in Britain mean for those who experience it? In this section we give details of four households that live, by British definitions, in poverty. The names have been changed to protect people's identity, but the cases are real, and the income figures are actual for the winter period of 1986–7.

Readers may well react as a first impression by feeling that the sums of money given as income seem quite substantial. They are adequate for survival, nothing more. Life on these levels of income allows for none of the so-called extras that bring choice, or joy. There is little fullness in a life lived on Supplementary Benefit, and hope and dignity are further drained by the very process of having to apply for the benefits in question, and prove one's need.

1   Mr and Mrs Alexander

Mr Alexander receives basic Supplementary Benefit for his family. In addition, he receives diet additions for Mrs Alexander who is diabetic, and for one daughter who suffers from a bowel disorder. Both have to adhere strictly to their diets. There are five children, one of whom is physically handicapped, and all of whom are bedwetters which means that Mrs Alexander has to do three extra washes a day. An allowance is given of 60 pence for each wash to cover the cost of electricity, soap powder, and disinfectant. A higher heating addition is also paid along with an additional payment for wear and tear of clothes.

Mr Alexander receives the lower rate of Attendance Allowance because of the care required by the child who is physically handicapped and in addition receives fares to visit his elderly parents in hospital.

The total amount of benefit received by the Alexander family each week is

> £117.35 Normal requirement
> £ 63.92 Additional requirements
> (laundry, diet, heating etc.)
> _____
> £181.27

Because Mr Alexander already receives £35.00 Child Benefit, he is paid the balance of £146.27 as Supplementary Benefit. In addition, he receives £20.45 Attendance Allowance. As he is on Supplementary Benefit, all Mr Alexander's housing costs are paid through the Housing Benefit system.

Mrs Alexander is quite frail and the work of caring for the child who is handicapped falls mostly on Mr Alexander. He copes with this very cheerfully, giving attention to the other children as well and regularly visiting his parents. Managing on their income requires very strict budgeting, particularly because of the heating, the special diets and the replacement of clothing and bedding. While they appreciate the additional allowances, they do not in fact meet the additional expenditure. It becomes obvious as one looks at the tasks of caring for this family that it would be impossible for Mrs Alexander to cope if her husband were not unemployed and at home. By being there and taking responsibility, he is doing a very important job of work though that is not recognized. If he were not working within the family, it would be costing the State very much more in residential and domiciliary services.

The family have never been on holiday together, none of the children have been in a motor car, or seen a cow, or the seaside, though they are aware through their rented television set that the world is full of interesting possibilities.

Mr Alexander buys a newspaper every day. He has one evening off a week when he goes with a friend to the pub and has two pints of beer. He buys one round, his friend buys the other. Neither he nor his wife expect to get new clothes for themselves – jumble sales and Oxfam provide their wardrobes. The children's clothes are mostly second hand but it is not always possible to get second hand shoes so those are a special source of worry. So are festivals like Christmas and birthdays. They can never give each other anything and the idea no longer occurs to them but they try to make sure that each child gets what it wants, particularly at Christmas. They have no sense of being sorry for themselves but they are aware that their children are not having the opportunities they would have wanted for them.

2   *Miss Brown*

Miss Brown is 77 and lives alone. She suffers from angina, chronic bronchitis, arthritis and is unable to leave her house. She had reluctantly retired at 60 from a clerical job to which she had devoted her emotional life, and managed, while she was active, to keep busy and live on her tiny retirement pension. As she became progressively disabled, she began to draw on her small savings, particularly to meet heating bills. Her savings had already been eroded because she had been the sole support of her own mother until her death when Miss Brown was in her late fifties. Miss Brown had her State Pension but until contacted by a welfare rights worker, as a result of a house survey, had never considered herself the kind of person who was entitled to any extra financial help.

Her income at that time was a total of £52 per week. From that she was paying rent and rates of £35, leaving £17 for food, heating, laundry, cleaning materials, clothes and tips to local children who did her shopping for her. She had no relatives who could have helped.

Intervention by the welfare rights worker resulted in increases amounting to £56 per week. This includes an attendance allowance, an age-related heating addition for being over 70, plus additions for laundry, baths and wear and tear of clothing. She was also awarded single payments for clothing and bedding.

Miss Brown had been living below the poverty line for many years. She had no television set, nor did she take a daily newspaper. From either of these she might have learned that she was entitled to help from Social Security. She, and others like her, are dependent on local authorities or voluntary organizations having enough funds to recruit staff to make house-to-house calls or to run campaigns which will inform any professionals or members of the general public who might come into contact with people living in isolation.

3   Mr Hill

Mr Hill, a widower aged 36, has 5 children. His income totals £74.17 weekly, which is made up of £53.17 Supplementary Benefit and £21.00 Family Allowance. His wife died suddenly one year ago and he has tried to keep the family together rather than have them go into care. In spite of this, the two youngest children were considered to be in need of care and were temporarily fostered but have now been returned.

The correct level of Family Allowance was not reinstated for some months and he was forced to apply for a grant for clothing to the Social Work Department. This was given but it is becoming increasingly difficult for the Local Authority to provide this kind of grant. The children are aged between 18 months and 10 years, ages which are most demanding for parents both emotionally and financially. The eldest is mentally handicapped and attends special school. This child has been particularly distressed since the loss of his mother and at home is destructive of his clothes and aggressive to the other children.

Mr Hill is very good with the children and tries to act as a substitute mother, doing housework, cooking and caring for them. He has very little family support but the Social Work Department provides part-time home help and child minding for the two youngest children. He has had a disturbed personal history of heavy drinking and a number of suicide attempts leading to a period of hospitalization while his wife was alive. It was she who provided the stability and ability to manage their very limited resources.

It is now clear that the home is becoming steadily bleaker and the children more deprived of emotional warmth, intellectual stimulation and fun. Mr Hill's anxiety about his capacity to manage financially is intensifying, the breakdown of the washing machine or the hoover presents him with a seemingly insoluble crisis. Social Work staff involved with the family are increasingly concerned about his ability to hold the home together. If these children were to be taken into care the cost to the community would be considerably more than the provision of domiciliary services.

4   The Macpherson family

The family consists of Mr and Mrs Macpherson both in their mid-30s and four children aged 15, 14, 13 and 5.

They live in a four-apartment upper flat rented from the Local Authority. It is situated in an area of pre-war housing which is noted for poor housing standards, low income families, poor standards of repairs and maintenance, high unemployment. . .

Mr Macpherson has been unemployed for some years. He is unskilled and has little prospect of future employment in the present economic climate. The family are in receipt of Supplementary Benefit of £132 per fortnight and Child Benefit of £28 per week. Although there are no major debts or arrears, it is recognized that this has been achieved as a result of major household items not being replaced. As a result, the house is barely furnished, with little in the way of comfort.

There are three teenagers in the family, all of whom have healthy appetites. Mrs Macpherson finds it difficult to stretch her budget to provide them with sufficient quantity and quality of food to satisfy their hunger all the time. A similar problem exists in relation to the replacement of clothes and footwear for a swiftly growing family.

The children are very aware that fashionable clothes are

not possible within the family budget. They resent this and are conscious that they look different from many of their peers. The two eldest children have been involved in minor offences within the community and have experienced difficulty in school, in part regarding behaviour and attitude, but mainly in respect of attendance. It is considered that lack of adequate clothing caused them shame and embarrassment at school and contributed significantly to their poor attendance record.

Mr and Mrs Macpherson both recognize the benefits for their children in taking part in activities outside the home. The eldest child is a keen swimmer, the second keen to play football, but the family's restricted budget does not allow for this on a regular basis. Consequently much of the family's time is spent watching TV or playing pool at home.

The family feel their low income status very keenly. There is an air of depression around the home and it is clear that the parents view themselves as being totally powerless in the situation. They have little positive contact with extended family or within the neighbourhood and have become increasingly insular and inward-looking.

The children too lack confidence in themselves. Their verbal skills are poor and they are socially inept. Like their parents, they are conscious of the family's low income and their lack of status. They seem to react in a flat depressed manner, punctuated by occasional outbursts of resentment and anger.

Mr Macpherson's self-image has been damaged by his inability to provide adequately for his family through his unemployment. Mrs Macpherson's self-confidence is similarly low. She regards herself as inadequate because she is unable to provide her family with basic necessities, such as food and clothing. Both see lack of money as their main problem, but cannot see a way out for them or for their children. Their abilities as parents have been questioned as a result of problems at school and in the community, with a consequent loss of confidence in their own parenting skills.

Their confidence, skills and standards have been eroded by their dependence on state benefits.

This family, which is basically competent and would be coping perfectly well if jobs were available, demonstrates significantly the problem of the sense of exclusion and personal failure that derives from living at poverty levels. Their financial poverty embodies the essential elements of poverty in the 80s – poverty of *expectation*, of *opportunity* and of *choice*. Not only are the members of this family poor but they feel poor, they are constantly aware of the humiliation of their position, a humiliation which is constantly compounded by their exposure through television to standards of consumption which appear to be taken for granted by the rest of the community.

A particular humiliation is experienced by parents who feel failure in being unable to give their children those toys and clothes which are appropriate to their age and stage of development. In some families it is this sense of failure that becomes converted to anger which, for lack of an appropriate outlet, can be turned against the children who become symbols of the parental failure.

5   Bombay contrasts

Like any city, Bombay has its rich and poor, and those in between. However, as a 'Third World' megapolis, and more so because it grew up on a peninsula, Bombay's affluent minority and its millions of ill-housed working classes are crowded close together, with what we would call the middle class forming a relatively small group between them. Compare two young men, *Dilip* and *Suresh*, living there, about a mile apart, unknown to each other and unlikely ever to meet.

Dilip ran away from a village home in 1976 when he was 14, travelling (without a ticket) by train the 300 miles from his home to the freedom of the bright lights. A year later he had lost his left leg while 'self–employed' on the local trains. He used to get up from the pavement where he slept outside the main station, early enough to sneak on the first local passenger train, and then sit on a seat until the compartment got so crowded that some desperate commuter paid him ten paise (1p) or so for it. At the terminus he would repeat the process. You have to be good at jumping from carriage to carriage on a moving train to avoid the railway police and one day ... After that Dilip cleaned taxis and became adept at using a staff to get round on one leg, sleeping on a traffic island outside Victoria Terminal with a group of sixty or so other young folk whose leader he had become.

Suresh over these years had grown up at home, in a house which came with his father's job, sharing one of the bedrooms with his brother and going to an expensive English-medium school where he excelled at sport. Like most of his year, he passed enough Highers to go on to the best college in Bombay, run like the school by the Jesuit order. By 1978 he was doing a post-graduate Master's in Business Administration.

That year Dilip had started to sell black-market cinema tickets. Films being very popular, it pays an enterprising manager to put 'House Full' notices outside and pass the tickets out through a middleman to boys who sell them, marked-up, to eager patrons, then hand the proceeds back to their minder who pays them the price of a meal, pays the local policeman a retainer to look the other way, and gives the cinema manager a better turnover. Arrests are occasionally arranged to make clear the disapproval of the authorities but the boys are soon released when the minder makes a suitable donation to the badly-paid police sergeant, and this is naturally recovered by instalments from the boys concerned, giving them an incentive to stick at the job. Dilip had at least two spells in jail.

By 1982, Suresh had landed a well-paid post with an advertising agency handling accounts for multinationals marketing detergents and music centres. Soon after that, his family arranged an excellent marriage, to Rohini, 'fair-complexioned, good-looking, 158 cm, Bombay BA, caste no bar', as the advert in one Sunday's *Times of India* put it.

Dilip had also done well in his terms, with enough saved up to buy a small stock of cigarettes and matches to set up with a couple of boxes as a stall on some open ground near the roundabout. Maya, a small, lively, dark brown girl lived with him and they took great pride in a little baby daughter.

Today Suresh clears around £400 a month and he and Rohini have a nice three-roomed flat in Kozi Hom Apartments. Their son will be starting at the Little Flower Nursery School soon and his name is down for the school his father went to, though they would like to move to the States if the right opening comes.

Maya died in 1984 but Dilip still has his small stall, their child and usually a smile for his customers. He sleeps on the ground by the boxes at night. Daily profits do not quite reach £1 but it is enough to live on and, after all, many of his mates are still saving seats on trains or selling those cinema tickets.

C. Comments from Easterhouse

Our 'testimonies' were by educated and privileged people, deeply affected by knowing something of poverty around them. Our 'cases' brought us face to face with the realities facing individual poor people. But the poor are well able to speak their own truth. What follows is not really dialogue as much as interwoven statements by two women who experience the reality of poverty in Easterhouse. They, and others like them, bear the brunt of maldistribution in our society today. There has been minimal editing of what they had to say.

Jean: I'm on Supplementary Benefit and on Monday I received £65.24 and on a Tuesday I have my Family Allowance of £21.30. Usually by the Thursday it's all gone. There's food in the cupboard but that's about it.

I have three children, my oldest one is 15, the middle one 11 (both boys), the youngest is 8, my daughter. The heaviest expenditure? Oh I don't really know ... clothing and then the weekly food. I need about four cows tethered in the garden to keep them going on milk! Foodstuff is the main weekly thing but it always happens that all three happen to need shoes at just about the same time. Christmas is just a nightmare, a total nightmare, you've got to get into debt and that generates having less money for maybe six months because you're paying off the last Christmas.

It really is quite easy to get into debt, too easy actually. At the moment I have my own mail order catalogue, which is very expensive.

But then again you are given time to pay them. There is the Provident personal credit who give you credit cheque books so that you can go to the shops and buy things for your kids. That is mostly how I clothe my children, which takes a sizeable chunk of your money every week.

Every week I pay £11.00 between my catalogue and the cheques. It has been more, it has been less, but at the moment I am paying £11.00 a week.

Philomena: I do agree with what Jean is saying in that poverty is lack of this, that and the other, shoes, clothes, food and things like that. But when I look at poverty, I look at a different perspective altogether. Poverty, real poverty to me is basically a lack of awareness, or a lack of education, which I think is more important. I think that if people could become more aware, if people could become more educated then probably people wouldn't suffer poverty as much as we do today.

I had two friends, Janet and David, and they had three children and Janet and her husband were quite heavy drinkers and they were always, always fighting and her husband was always beating her up, and she was always covered in bruises, never where you could see them, always on the body. And Janet used to come over quite often to talk. 'Oh he's just beat me up again', and we just used to talk about it and I tried to make her understand that perhaps if the two of them could get some help about the drinking it would be better. It seemed it was only when they drank that the problems came to the fore and they couldn't talk about problems for fighting about the problems. The drink was one of the main reasons why they couldn't cope and because they couldn't cope they would turn to more drink and then things would just get worse and worse, so I was trying to say that if they could just try and understand that the drinking causes them to have less money, because they are spending it on drink, then they've got less money and they can't pay the bills, then the bills just get bigger and bigger and the problems just get bigger and bigger and because of the problems they just turned back to drink again, its just like a vicious circle. If they could just understand that if they could get their priorities right, stop drinking first and then they would have more money to start paying the bills off and once they started paying the bills off the pressure would come down a bit more and they wouldn't argue so much, they would get on a lot better, and then they wouldn't need to turn to drink as much. That's just an example, a small example.

But the unfortunate thing that happened to the two of them was things just got worse and they just got deeper and deeper into debt and they got worse and worse with the drink and it ended up one night the two of them died in a fire because they were so drunk. I mean, this is what poverty leads to.

Jean: I don't sit and say 'Oh my God I'm poverty stricken'. I mean, you live in poverty, you make the best out of it. There are people round about me, Oh God, there is one woman that it just breaks my heart to see her, she's always walking about in what looks like second-hand type jumble sale clothes, and she has a squad of kids. I mean she has six or seven kids. Every night, it must be degrading for the children as well, but every night she walks the streets, okay if she walks the street, the kids walk about her in a circle and she just looks as if she's taking a leisurely walk and the kids are picking the douts, the cigarette ends, off the ground for the mum to smoke later on. Now that to me is ten thousand times worse than anything I have been through, and I've been through quite a bit. I think you try to hide the poverty from the kids, because when you're a kid you don't say 'Oh my God, I'm poor', you know, you don't feel poverty. Ask any kid that was brought up in Easterhouse, do they feel poor, twenty years on, and they'll say no, I had a great life, we were out playing with our pals all the time. I mean it didn't matter if there was dog shit on the pavement or broken bottles lying about. We were kids, we loved that. I think it's a state of mind, okay you don't have money, but that's only one thing that you need to keep going. I'll guarantee you that I am a lot happier than a lot of people with lots of money.

Phil: I moved into Easterhouse when Lesley was a baby. I was on my own, I was very depressed. I'd already had one breakdown. I was in the house every day and all day long. when Lesley was three, she went to nursery and I was alone all day long. I didn't have any friends – I was very quiet, very reserved – and I used to feel as if the walls were coming in on me. My brother told me about the Festival Society and suggested I go and try to become involved. I thought about it for weeks and weeks, then one day I sat down and said to myself, 'Now Phil, this is what you've got ... you've got a child, a house, you don't have enough money to get yourself out, you've got no friends, no future, you can either stay here for the rest of your life or you can pluck up your courage and get out there. Go and see, just go and take a look.' So I did. I went into the office one day and said 'I'm Phil, Peter's sister.' They made me welcome and I felt at home straight away. I used to do things like make the coffee because I was very quiet, then I progressed a wee bit to answering the phones which I was very conscious about since I was deaf, then hand printing, then a wee bit typing and eventually anything that needed to be done.

I've always managed reasonably well financially. It's easier having one child. I've never been one for allowing myself to go into debt. The only debt I was in was the electricity and I was a wee bit late in paying and they cut it off.

I think it's disgusting the price of electricity. They knew that I was screwing the meter before I started paying it direct. I can't stand a cold place, and I don't think it's right that people with children or even people on their own should live in a cold house, particularly in winter time. I'm also inclined to be anaemic. I've got some disease in my blood so that I feel the cold a lot. And I was also very aware of the cold when putting my wee one to her bed. I thought, I'm just going to have to do it, I can't bear this cold, I'm going to have to do something with the meter. And I did. I got it done and I don't care much about it. At first I couldn't sleep for months and I was scared stiff in case the electricity man came to the door. But now I don't think much about it at all.

Jean: Oh, it's all important to have friends, it's really and truly all important you know. We're really lucky with the Festival Society, that sort of group that we are at the moment, because we're not just friends, we're like family. I mean, Teresa's like my sister, so is Margaret, so is everybody. I can go to them if I'm down and they can come to me if they're down. We share a lot of the stress and a lot of strain.

Phil: The church should be teaching people the truth about God. Everything's its business. I don't think the churches should stay strictly to religion. I think also before anyone tries to bring the church into the community where it can deal with these issues like we're talking about, or other issues, I think it really should take a good look at itself, because I believe the churches are part of the reason why people suffer poverty. And we're not talking materialistic poverty, we're talking about religious poverty, God poverty, understanding, education, you know, because like I said earlier, churches make too many rules and regulations. It's a power-loaded thing and it sucks people so that the church can be strong, so that the church can take over, and it's really conning people in a sense because it's not giving people the truth. All these people who are priests, canons, bishops, are supposed to know about religion – they are poverty stricken, because they suffer from a lack of the truth in a sense of what God really is, what God really means to people and what God has really meant for people. Because God meant people to live in peace and harmony, but people don't live in peace and harmony, and part of the reason is that there are so many conflicts in the church itself.

Jean has just come through a kind of hell – her divorce, and then Helen had her breakdown, and I remember when Helen took the overdose she just wanted to die. To me, hell is a state of mind, and we can all be there. If we stopped being greedy and stopped being selfish and started looking after each other, then there would be heaven on earth. It's an ideal for the world to be happy but I think it's possible if you look at it like Janet and our friends. They're all different individuals who all have their own problems who have come together and grown – all these years – and we've grew into a family.

To my family, I am a sinner, because I have a kid and I'm not married. But they didn't ask why I had a breakdown, they don't come and visit me. My mother said 'You've made your bed, you'll lie in it.' And that was a kind of poverty, so poverty's a whole lot of different things.

Chapter Two

DISTRIBUTION TODAY: PATTERNS AND TRENDS

Behind the experiences described in the previous chapter lie patterns of distribution of which many people are singularly unaware. The patterns are complex and often not easy to understand. But what is obvious is that there are 'winners' and 'losers', and that the way things are distributed and the trends in distribution raise great issues of justice and fairness.

Before we move to interpretation we need to consider the facts – how wealth, income and benefits are in fact distributed in Britain today, and the way things are moving. In order to put these things in their proper context we will have a little to say about global distribution, although this is in its own right a major issue which deserves far more extended treatment than we can give it here. We present the facts with the minimum of interpretation or evaluation. Taken along with the human situations outlined in chapter one, the facts are cause for concern, perhaps even for dismay and anger. The challenge they present to our ideas of justice, love and neighbourliness we turn to in chapter three.

1 What is poverty?

Some people still assume that poverty simply involves not having the resources to sustain biological life – food, shelter, clothing, and so on: 'A family is poor if it cannot afford to eat' (Joseph and Sumption, 1979, 27–28). People, according to this definition, are poor when they are below a subsistence level. However, this is to treat human beings as little more than biological organisms, instead of recognizing that they are social beings who have feelings and beliefs and are part of a system of relationships which gives them a sense of identity and worth. There are major problems involved in developing any objective standard of poverty which is independent of the values and attitudes of people in a particular society and culture and period of time.

For poverty, like wealth, is a relative term, defined in and by a culture and a society. People are wealthy, or poor, in comparison with other people in the same society; the social values recognized by a society prescribe what is acceptable and what is unacceptable in terms of wealth and poverty. It is an outrage that so many people die of starvation in a world that has in other countries vast unused food surpluses. But that does not mean that we should be unconcerned that so many of our fellow-citizens have poor health, much reduced life expectancy, less choice and fewer life chances than the rest of us because they are poor – not in the absolute sense that they are starving, but poor compared with the rest of us, living at a level that we would find quite unacceptable for ourselves or our own children.

Successive governments have recognized that there is in fact a level of income below which people should not be allowed to sink, or in other words, that there is an unacceptable level of poverty. As a kind of rule of thumb the Supplementary Benefit rate may be used, and is used by government agencies, as a poverty line. But this is determined in part by what government feels it can afford rather than by any careful assessment of what is needed to ensure a decent standard of life. And it is very commonly accepted today that those with net resources below 140% of the Supplementary Benefit scale should be regarded as being on the margins of poverty. Peter Townsend in his classic study, *Poverty in the United Kingdom*, suggested that there was a 'poverty threshold' at around 150% of the Supplementary Benefit rate. Below this level deprivation increased sharply; above it deprivation decreased steadily.

More recently in the study *Poor Britain*, Mack and Lansley have developed an approach to identifying the poor which tries to resolve some criticisms made of Townsend's study, especially concerning the choices people make on how to spend their money. They conducted a survey to discover whether there is any consensus in Britain as to what may be a minimum level of acceptable living in terms of material circumstances. This was done by asking a representative sample of the population to choose from a list of items those which they regarded as necessary for a decent way of life in Britain today. There was remarkable agreement across social classes and political alignments. It was also found that as income fell, access to the agreed list of necessities fell most sharply when income went below about 150% of the Supplementary Benefit scale. Here was an income threshold below which deprivation increased sharply. Thus the study demonstrated that there is a broadly held consensus in Britain that families with less than about 150% of the Supplementary Benefit level of income are poor and steps should be taken to improve their situation. So official agencies, the researches of people like Peter Townsend, and the opinions of most people in Britain agree in seeing about 150% of the Supplementary Benefit rate as the threshold of poverty.

At present (March 1987), the weekly short-term SB rate for a single householder, excluding housing costs, is £29.80. For a married couple it is £48.40, and for a couple with two children aged eight and twelve, £73.90. By way of contrast, the average household income in the United Kingdom is approximately £190 per week.

Poverty, of course, is not simply a matter of lack of money. As David Donnison and others argue, 'poverty means a standard of living so low that it excludes people from the community in which they live' (Donnison, 1982, 7). Donnison wrote in the SBC Report for 1978:

> To keep out of poverty, people must have an income which enables them to participate in the life of the community. They must be able, for example, to keep themselves reasonably fed, and well enough dressed to maintain their self-respect and to attend interviews for jobs with

confidence. Their homes must be reasonably warm; their children should not feel shamed by the quality of their clothing; the family must be able to visit relatives, and give them something on their birthdays and at Christmas time; they must be able to read newspapers, and retain their television sets and their membership of trade unions and churches. And they must be able to live in a way which ensures, so far as possible, that public officials, doctors, teachers, landlords and others treat them with the courtesy due to every member of the community (Donnison, 1982, 8).

This understanding of poverty as exclusion is a reminder that poverty has clear social and indeed spiritual dimensions and implications. Poverty can do great damage to families and individuals. And a society which tolerates poverty cannot be regarded as spiritually or morally healthy. The way a society distributes its resources is a symptom of its ethical and spiritual vitality.

2   The growth of poverty in Britain

Since 1979 the number of people in Britain living at or below the Supplementary Benefit level – that is to say the state's own assessment of the income required to sustain the lowest living standard at which any member of society should be expected to live – has increased dramatically, from 6.1 to 8.9 million persons; from 11.5% to 16.6% of the population. Although there has been a slight fall in pensioner poverty since 1979, the incidence remains high: 3.0 million people of whom 2.0 million live alone. This means that a third of all pensioners live in poverty.

Poverty within families under pension age has doubled, from 3.0 to 6.0 million persons (6.8% to 13.3%). There is much evidence of an increase in child poverty, although families with and without children all registered increases in poverty. Single parent families are especially liable to be poor with more than half in receipt of Supplementary Benefit. There has also been a notable increase among families with three or more children, where the incidence of poverty rose from 10.8% to 22.0%, the families in question now involving 1.4 million people. Those who live in families with children now make up a quarter of the poor (26.2%) compared to 16.1% in 1979.

Unemployment is the main cause of increased poverty. No less than three quarters of people in the families of the unemployed live in poverty. These numbers trebled between 1979 and 1983, from 1.0 million to 3.1 million. The unemployed and their families now make up nearly a third of the poor (31.9%), compared to 16.1% in 1979. In 1979 over half of the poor came from pensioner families, by 1983 this had fallen to a third. Some 20% of persons in families of the sick and disabled live in poverty.

It is one thing to live for a week, or perhaps for a month or two, on or below the Supplementary Benefit level. But when this stretches to a year, two years, three years or more, it must be regarded as totally unacceptable in a decent society. Long-term poverty is particularly serious for the families of the unemployed, who are the only group who are barred from receiving the higher rate of Supplementary Benefit after twelve months on the basic rate. Pensioners receive the higher rate from the start, and other applicants after a year.

In Scotland in February, 1985, 506,000 people, that is 9.6% of the population, were in direct receipt of supplementary benefits. When one adds the dependents to this we have a figure of 797,000 which is 15.4% of the population, as compared with 8.2% in 1979. When one adds to the 1985 figures the people on Family Income Supplement and those eligible who do not claim, we get a percentage of Scots living at or below the Supplementary Benefit level of 18.7. Those with an income of between 100% and 140% of Supplementary Benefit level add another 12.9%, giving a figure for the total number of Scots living in poverty or on the margins of poverty in 1985 of 1,641,000 or 31.7% of the population (SCCVO, 1986). In Scotland, as in the UK as a whole, the greatest increase in Supplementary Benefit recipients has come among the unemployed and single-parent families.

Table 1: Scotland's Poor 1985*

1   How many people depend on supplementary benefits? ('000s)

	Main categories of recipients of regular weekly payments			Other recipients	All recipients	Total number of dependants inc. recipients	Average % of Scottish population
	Supplementary pensioners	Unemployed recipients	Single-parent recipients				
1973 (Nov)	182	46	21	40	289	392	7.5
1979 (Nov)	151	79	32	24	286	425	8.2
1982 (Nov)	150	192	45	36	423	702	13.5
1985 (Feb)	149	219	50	88	506	797	15.4

(estimated)

2   How many people depend on incomes which qualify them for supplementary benefit but do not claim them?

163   (3.1)

3   How many people are in receipt of Family Income Supplement (FIS), or eligible for it, whose gross incomes are below supplementary benefit rates?

10   (0.19)

Total living at or below supplementary benefit rates   970   18.7

4   How many people are dependent on incomes between 100% and 140% of supplementary benefit level?

671   (12.9)

5   Total number of Scots living in poverty or on the margins of poverty

1,641,000   31.7

* Taken from Scottish Council of Community and Voluntary Organisations Briefing Paper, *Poverty in Scotland*, 1986

Scotland has a higher proportion of recipients of Supplementary Benefit payments than the rest of Britain, and social security benefits provide a higher proportion of gross household income in Scotland than in other parts of Britain – in 1983 18.7% as against a UK average of 14.9%.

How are we to understand the continuance and growth of poverty in a wealthy nation with a developed social security system? A number of factors may combine to allow poverty even when the adults are in full-time work, such as low pay, a low level of child benefit which does not reflect the actual cost of children and low levels and poor take-up of Family Income Supplement and Housing Benefit. For those out of work, the level of national insurance benefit paid is inadequate, especially for pensioners and families with children, and the duration of benefit is too short, especially for the unemployed. As a result significant numbers have become dependent for long periods upon means-tested Supplementary Benefit, with its attendant problems of stigma and take-up. In 1948, one in thirty-three of the population were dependent on means-tested Supplementary Benefit; today it is one in eight.

For those who have assumed that the Welfare State has abolished real poverty, the facts come as a surprise and a shock. The fact is that the Beveridge Scheme rested on a number of assumptions which no longer hold true. It assumed that when a man was in work, his pay would be sufficient for himself, his wife and their first child. It assumed that the wife would not work but would be dependent on her husband, and that in sickness, unemployment or retirement, people would have a benefit or pension based on their insurance contribution record. Until such time as an adequate insurance scheme was fully established there would be a safety net of means-tested assistance whose importance would decline over time.

But Beveridge did not anticipate that there would be so much poverty arising from low pay in work, nor did he foresee the vast growth of unemployment, especially long-term unemployment. The initial levels of benefits through

National Insurance were set too low and never adequately upgraded and as a result when National Assistance (later Supplementary Benefit) levels were increased, more and more people drifted on to means-tested assistance, rather than obtaining benefits as of right. Meanwhile, forms of private welfare grew, especially in the form of occupational pensions and fringe benefits, and substantial tax allowances and relief were available as a kind of 'exchequer subsidy' to higher income groups.

3 Distribution at the workplace

We can relate the distribution of earnings to the median point, that is, the point in the earnings distribution where half the workers have earnings above and half have earnings below that point. Thus, for example, in 1985 the lowest 10% of male earners had earnings that were 60.8% of the median for all male workers whereas the highest 10% of earners had 171.5% of the median.

Inequality of earnings for men has increased over the past ten years, and especially since 1980. The distribution has widened from the median at both top and bottom. This is true of all male workers, both manual and non-manual. The position of the lowest paid has got worse relative to both median earnings and earnings of the highest paid.

For women the dispersion of earnings narrowed between 1975 and 1980, but then widened again to 1985. Within this overall picture, pay of the lowest 10% of women manual workers has moved fractionally closer to the median. And women manual workers on the highest 10% of earnings improved their position.

There is clear evidence of a widening gap between the earnings of manual and non-manual men over the past ten years, especially since 1980. For women the gap widened only slightly between 1975 and 1980, but then increased sharply to 1985. As we shall see later, these growing inequalities of earnings between manual and non-manual workers are extended further by income from wealth and in the form of 'fringe benefits'.

One area in which inequality has declined is in the earnings of all women, compared to those of all men. The measure of low pay used here is two-thirds of median male earnings. In April 1985 this was £115 per week. The median was £172.80. Low pay has declined among women non-manual workers. Nevertheless, the earnings of most women are still only two-thirds that of men.

More people are low paid, particularly in Scotland, where the proportion of low paid among male manual workers has doubled since 1979, from 10.8% to 22.1%. Although there has been a fall in low pay among female non-manual workers, low pay among women remains at a very high level: three-quarters of all manual and half of all non-manual women workers are low paid.

In Scotland significant regional variations in low pay exist, and its overall level would be much higher but for overtime working. A quarter of all male workers in Scotland would be low paid were it not for overtime working. Overtime is especially important for male manual workers. For example, the incidence of low pay in Tayside would have risen from 31.0% to 50.6% but for overtime. Even in relatively prosperous Grampian overtime reduced low pay only from 33.5% to 20.1%. The worst regions for low pay among men are Tayside, Borders, Dumfries and Galloway, and Highland. 57.3% of all women are low paid; overtime has less effect in reducing low pay among women.

The estimated number of low paid workers in Scotland in 1985 was 903,000, which was 46.3% of all employees. Of that total 620,000 (69%) were women, and 370,000 (41%) were part-time employees (Smail 1986).

In their early years of employment male manual workers have earnings above those of non-manual male workers, but by their mid twenties they are overtaken. They reach a peak of earnings in their thirties, remain on a plateau through their forties and then their earnings decline, particularly sharply after their mid fifties.

By contrast, male non-manual workers' earnings continue to rise into their early fifties, although they too find earnings decline after sixty. Their steady rise in earnings is probably related to incremental pay scales that provide an automatic annual increase in pay separate from and in addition to the annual round of wage bargaining. Such automatic increases are not usually available to manual workers. The life-cycle of earnings for women is much flatter, for both manual and non-manual workers, with little improvement in average earnings after the late twenties, especially for women manual workers.

Since the mid nineteenth century governments have increasingly intervened in the labour market to control and discourage unduly low levels of pay and set standards of fair wages. The Fair Wages Resolution of 1891 can be regarded as fairly typical of a tradition within the Conservative Party which sees it as a social duty to intervene in market relations to protect groups of workers from the worst effects of uncontrolled market competition. It was introduced to deal with 'the evils of sweating'. The so-called sweated trades were subject to fierce competition among a multiplicity of small firms which were not unionized, and thus unregulated in their pay and conditions. The Resolution provided that employers operating government contracts should pay the wage generally accepted 'in each trade for competent workmen', thus invoking notions of fairness embodied in custom and practice. The legislation was strengthened by a Liberal government in 1909 to include hours and conditions of work, and was widened in its application by a Labour government in 1946. Thus, over a long period there has been an all-party consensus for ensuring minimum standards and wages at work. Harold Macmillan spoke of the Fair Wages Resolution as 'the great protector of the standard of life of the mass of the wage earning classes and of the long built tradition of co-operation within industry'. The Conservative government abolished the Fair Wages Resolution in 1983. Partly as a result, large groups of already low paid workers are finding their pay and conditions deteriorating still further – a matter of special concern to those who believe we should give special priority to the poorest groups in our society.

Another Act of Parliament established Wages Councils in 1909. The government recently contemplated their abolition but in face of opposition from both sides of industry allowed them to continue, but with reduced powers. Wages Councils comprise representatives of employers and unions, as well as independent members. They determine legal minimum rates of pay and conditions for three million workers in such jobs as catering, laundry, hairdressing and clothing manufacture. The employees covered are usually poorly unionized and often remain poorly paid since the minimum rates set are still very low. About three quarters are women who often work part-time or at home.

The Wages Councils system has its own problems. Enforcement of the minimum rates set has been poor. There are few Wages Inspectors and infrequent inspections. Noncompliance is high and the penalties for breaking the law are derisory. Yet the issue is a serious one, as Winston Churchill said when introducing the legislation in 1909:

> It is a serious national evil that any class of His Majesty's subjects should receive less than a living wage in return for their utmost exertions ... Where you have no organization, no parity of bargaining, the good employer is undercut by the bad and the bad employer by the worst ... where these conditions prevail you have not a condition of progress, but a condition of progressive degeneration.

Whether governments intervene or refuse to intervene, they are making judgments of a moral sort about the fairness and importance of relations of distribution. Poverty and low pay are the result of processes of distribution instigated or tolerated by governments and public opinion. Because they mean having less freedom and choice for oneself and one's family, they raise issues which are both ethical and spiritual.

4   *The poverty trap*

British governments, in as far as they have concerned themselves with wage levels, have usually focussed their attention upon the low paid. Unlike Scandinavian governments, they have not seen the *distribution* of earnings as a question which they should be concerned with, or a policy problem which ought to be publicly debated. In recent years, earnings have become increasingly unequal. Meanwhile workers with children to support have found that the value of Child Benefit in relation to their wages has fallen. Thus some low paid workers with several children, often labouring in very unattractive jobs, get less in wages and Child Benefit than they would receive if they were living on social security benefits which have to be sufficient to keep the family alive – and that seems unfair to most people. Britain has attempted to solve this problem by topping up the earnings of the 'working poor' with a growing array of means-tested benefits: Housing Benefit, Family Income Supplement, free school meals, free health service prescriptions, and so on.

These benefits work very badly because they are often felt to be humiliating: they are expensive to administer and too complex to understand – and therefore they achieve very low rates of take-up. (Only half the people entitled to Family Income Supplement actually get it, and the take-up rates for free school meals and some other means-tested benefits are lower still.) Meanwhile the tapering-out of these benefits as incomes rise, coupled with the tapering-in of Income Tax and National Insurance contributions creates the 'poverty trap' in which many of the working poor find themselves. Much of the public discussion of social security and social policies focusses on this poverty trap and the problems associated with it – the temptations it creates to fraud and the concealment of earnings, for example. Solutions to these problems cannot be found unless we confront their origins more frankly. These origins are the unequal distribution of pre-tax earnings and the inadequancy of child benefit and other forms of family support. With a pattern of earnings which is somewhat more equal and more adequate family support, we could begin to reduce Britain's reliance on means-tested benefits, abolishing Family Income Supplement and reducing housing benefits to a scale which could be more efficiently and fairly administered.

Many poor people are trapped in poverty because the tax and social security systems are working against each other. People are now liable to pay tax on incomes that are hardly above the official poverty line. The increased tax burden on those with below average earnings has combined with the extension of means testing (FIS and Housing Benefit) to produce the poverty trap for low paid workers.

Every £1 increase in earnings from work can be dramatically reduced by the combined loss of means-tested benefit and the additional payment of income tax and national insurance contributions. It is not surprising that there is discontent among the poor about levels of income tax; their treatment seems very unfair when compared with that of higher income groups, although they are probably unaware of the full extent of the inequities involved.

The 'poverty trap' may be illustrated as follows: from every additional pound earned there may be 27p deducted in Income Tax at the standard rate, together with between 5p and 9p deducted for National Insurance. The loss of Housing Benefit takes another 33p to 38p so that between 65p and 74p is lost from the additional pound earned. This loss on the part of the low paid may be contrasted with the top rate of income tax of 60p in the pound levied on the highest incomes. Thus the low paid worker has a higher effective marginal rate of income loss than the best paid worker in the land. And for some the position is worse than that illustrated.

The 'poverty trap' may operate over a wide band of income to produce a kind of 'poverty plateau'. 'Effectively, what our tax/benefit system has achieved for *families with earnings in the bottom quarter of the income distribution* is the end of differentials in net disposable resources' (Walker, 1982, 11). That is, whatever the increase in their earnings, they end up having the same amount to spend. This means that increases in take-home pay are hard to achieve, there are few incentives, and an escape from the poverty trap is all but impossible. 'The poverty plateau,' Walker claimed, 'is about the morality of the government encouraging workers to work harder and to claim means-tested benefits, when the combined effect may simply trap them into poverty' (Walker, 1982, 11). It is difficult to see any moral or economic justification for this situation. 'If it was widely realized it would surely cause an outrage' (Deacon and Bradshaw, 1983, 157).

Although a number of means-tested benefits existed earlier, it was primarily the new means-tested benefits introduced between 1970 and 1974 (Family Income Supplement, 1971, Rent Rebates in 1972 and 1973) which established the modern 'poverty trap'. For a generation we have taken pride in Britain in the rights of citizenship embodied in the Keynes/ Beveridge reforms of the welfare state. They were intended to give everyone the right to a proper level of income without the demeaning means tests of the pre-war years. This right has recently been undermined by increasing dependence on means-tested assistance.

5 Taxation and private welfare

Because we are encouraged to conceive of the tax system as a burden, we often overlook its powerful role in sharing, in distribution.

There have been several general changes in the impact of taxation since the war. There has been a shift from taxes on personal wealth and the corporate sector towards personal income tax. There has been an increase in the proportion of tax revenue raised through indirect taxes such as VAT which are levied without regard to the resources of the people paying. The new Community Charge in Scotland will be a local tax of this kind, unlike the old domestic rates which were related to the value of the property occupied. Within income tax there has been a shift over the last three decades towards poorer members of the community. A number of factors have brought this about:

(i) The system of tax allowances and reliefs has brought special benefits to higher income groups, as a byproduct of the extension of owner occupation, the growth of occupational pensions, and private health insurance, together with the charitable status of private education.

(*ii*) The value of personal tax allowances and of tax-free child benefits has declined.

(*iii*) The tax threshold has fallen. By way of illustration, in 1982 a couple with two children under eleven, with only the husband working, would have reached the tax threshold at half average earnings. Twenty-five years earlier no tax would have been paid until well above average earnings.

(*iv*) These changes have been worse for families with children than for single people or for couples without children.

(*v*) As a result of the removal of the reduced rate tax bands below the basic rate, we have the situation that while the level of income at which families pay tax has fallen, the rate at which they start to pay tax on entry to the tax system has increased. Hence the marginal rate of tax for those on less than average earnings has roughly trebled, while those on average earnings and above have seen little change in their marginal rate of tax in more than twenty-five years.

The vast bulk of Income Tax cuts have been concentrated on those at the very top of the income scale. Nearly half (45%) of all cuts since 1979 have gone to those in the top 10% of the income distribution. The top 1% alone will receive £1.7 billion in tax cuts in 1985/6 compared with a total of £1.7 billion for all those in the bottom 50%. Altogether the top 10% have received nearly three times the amount of tax cuts given to those in the bottom 50% (Hansard, 23 April 1986, cols 176–8). Thus the trend towards greater inequality of pre-tax earnings which we discussed earlier has been reinforced by the tax cuts since 1979 to produce greater inequality of post–tax incomes. Throughout the post-war period the combined impact of the Income Tax and social security systems has not been significantly effective in redistributing income from higher to lower income groups. And the cuts in Income Tax since 1979 have disproportionately benefitted the highest income groups.

In understanding the impact of the tax system on people with different levels of income, a distinction has to be made between 'marginal' and 'average' rates of tax. The 'marginal' rate is the tax paid on each additional pound of taxable income: and the average rate is that paid over all a person's income. Not all income is taxed. Personal allowances are not taxed; and income spent for certain purposes is relieved of tax – mortgage interest payments and occupational pensions contributions, for instance, are free of tax. These tax allowances and reliefs are more valuable to a person the higher their marginal rate of tax. They are part of the system of 'fiscal welfare' that interlinks with 'occupational welfare' (like occupational pensions or company cars) to add to a person's immediate or future income. This is often called the 'private welfare state' which, for people on higher incomes, tops up income from work and for many people largely replaces the public welfare system of state pensions, the NHS, Housing Benefit and Family Income Supplement. It is not easy to see how this subsidizing from the public purse of facilities for the already prosperous can be justified.

Fringe benefits are forms of income in kind which employers make available to some or all of their employees. Many fringe benefits are in fact subsidised by the tax system. The benefits may include free or subsidised meals, sports facilities, goods at discount prices, rent-free housing and occupational pensions. With the partial exception of the last, these are usually available to all employees within a particular firm. Other benefits such as company cars, cheap loans, and private medical insurance, as well as many forms of bonus and profit sharing, are usually only available to executives. Some of these benefits, such as company cars, provide a way around the pay limits of successive incomes policies. And it can be demonstrated that fringe benefits disproportionately benefit those in high income occupations. Overall, fringe benefits make up about 20–25% of labour costs, and the cost to the employer increases with the income of the employee. Tax reliefs on fringe benefits reduce the tax base, so that only roughly half of all income is liable to tax. Thus fringe benefits represent a loss of tax revenue to the Exchequer and accentuate the inequality of the distribution of income. They can be seen as a kind of subsidy from the general body of tax payers to selected groups, usually with above average incomes.

6   The distribution of wealth

Wealth is very much less evenly distributed than income. There has been some movement towards a less unequal distribution of wealth since the war, but nothing like as marked as many people believe. Redistribution of wealth has been concentrated largely within the top quarter. The share of wealth owned by the top 1% of wealth holders fell from 33% to 20% between 1966 and 1983, but in the same period the wealth held by the bottom 50% of the population rose only from 3% to 4%, and it has actually declined from 5% in 1979 to 4% in 1983. The loss of wealth by the top 10% has not benefitted the bottom 50% of wealth owners but the group immediately below the top 10%.

Table 2:   Distribution of Personal Wealth in the United Kingdom*

Concentration of wealth among adult population. Percentage of wealth owned by:	1966	1979	1983
	%	%	%
Top 1%	33	22	20
Next 1%	9	6	7
3–5%	14	12	13
6–10%	13	14	14
11–25%	18	23	24
26–50%	10	18	18
Top 50%	97	95	96
Bottom 50%	3	5	4
Top 25%	87	77	78
Bottom 75%	13	23	22

* Derived from Table 4.8, Inland Revenue Statistics, HMSO 1984 and Table 4.7, Inland Revenue Statistics, HMSO 1985.

The wealth of the poorer 50% of the population does not appear as yet to have been significantly affected by the development of so-called 'popular capitalism', and in particular by the growth of owner occupation, the sale of council houses, and the broader distribution of shares.

The importance of the distribution of wealth relates not

only to *how much* wealth is owned, but *what kind* of wealth is in question. A useful distinction may be made between what may be called 'domestic wealth' (dwellings, household goods, etc.) and 'production wealth' (land, shares, government securities, etc.). The distribution of 'production wealth' is especially important for it not only provides unearned income but it brings with it special power and influence within society. Where the ownership of 'production wealth' is concentrated in the hands of a few individuals and financial institutions, it involves a concentration of power which can cause problems in a democratic society. Ownership of 'production wealth' is far more concentrated than 'domestic wealth'. We have far to go before Britain can be regarded as a 'property-owning democracy' in which there is an equitable distribution of the kind of power and influence that goes with 'production wealth'.

Due to a number of tax advantages, housing has become one of the most profitable investments for ordinary people. The generous tax subsidy to those who can afford to buy becomes more valuable the higher the income and marginal tax rate of the purchaser. This has been well documented in a number of recent reports. This money foregone by the Exchequer is not counted as 'public expenditure' – unlike monies for Housing Benefit, which go to the poor. While the overall value of this tax subsidy to house owners has doubled to £4,750 million since 1979 (partly as a consequence of council house sales), the value of Housing Benefit for those on low incomes has declined as has the level of general expenditure on public sector housing.

Although a large section of the population lacks any significant wealth, there has been a more equitable distribution of 'domestic wealth' since the war. This can increase the freedom and quality of life for the possessors of 'domestic wealth'. But 'production wealth' remains concentrated in a small number of hands, and brings with it very great power.

7   Instruments of distribution

Distribution does not happen accidentally, but as the result of the working of instruments or mechanisms which may operate in a more or less impersonal way but are none the less subject to human control and designed by human beings. In other words, we are *responsible* for the patterns of distribution in our society, and given the will we can change them.

A few of the more important instruments of distribution, some of which have appeared earlier, will be briefly noted here.

(*a*) *The Welfare State*   Many recent studies have shown the institutions which are together commonly labelled the Welfare State to have been far less successful in eliminating poverty and inequality than had popularly been believed. Julian Le Grand demonstrated that in the key areas of health care, education, housing and transport, public expenditure had on the whole favoured the better off rather than the poor (Le Grand, 1982). More recently the Anglican Report, *Not Just for the Poor* (BSR, 1986) has confirmed this conclusion. Prosperous people are better able to make use of the facilities of the National Health Service. They find it easier to get access to better quality secondary education and to use this to get into further and higher education. In the housing field, as we have seen, owner-occupiers get more benefit from mortgage interest tax relief than do council tenants from rent subsidies. The social security system was – and is – extremely complex and confusing, so that many people do not know the benefits to which they are entitled. And the publicity given to a few 'benefit scroungers' who manage to 'play the system' has obscured the fact that there is a low take-up of many benefits on the part of people who really need them. As a mechanism of distribution there are serious problems in the present structure of the welfare state – problems which, in our opinion, have been made worse rather than solved by the Fowler reforms.

(*b*) *The tax system*   Facts and figures given earlier in this chapter give cause for concern on the part of those who believe that one of the functions of a just tax system is that it should favour the poor and attempt to eliminate poverty. The heaviest burdens, surely, should be borne by the broadest backs. But only too often the tax system in fact favours the rich, and it is only the prosperous who can devote attention and resources to tax avoidance, 'playing the tax system'. And as we have seen, sometimes the tax and statutory welfare systems seem to operate on different and contradictory principles so that benefits are, as it were, cancelled out. Or another and quite different state-subsidized welfare system is constructed alongside the statutory institutions of the welfare state. There is surely a pressing need for co-ordination between these two arms of public policy.

(c) *Public expenditure*   In spite of all their efforts, the Conservative governments since 1979 have not succeeded in reducing public expenditure *as a proportion of the national product*. In fact it was a higher percentage in 1986 than it was in 1979. Substantial and painful cuts have been made in spending on housing, education, especially higher education and some other areas, but spending has increased on defence and law and order, and also on the health services, though here it has lagged seriously behind the increased medical needs of an ageing population with high levels of unemployment and poverty. The cost of social security has risen because of the need to provide for growing numbers of old people, single parents, the chronic sick and, above all, over three million unemployed. The impact of many, if not all, cuts in public expenditure and attempts to limit necessary increases in spending on health care, and so on, falls disproportionately on the poor.

(d) *The market*   Our economy is basically a market system, although it works within a powerful framework of government activity and regulation. The market has advantages as a mode of distribution: it is flexible, with its own adjustment mechanisms; it offers choice to the consumer; it can channel self-interest so that it serves the common good. But the market is not a device for distributing *fairly*. Modern markets tend to be dominated by huge economic units which can

sometimes manipulate markets and effectively fix prices. On
the international scene, for example, it has been argued by
Raoul Prebisch and Hans Singer that the exports of developing countries – mainly commodities like coffee, copper, tea,
timber – buy less and less manufactured goods from the
industrial countries because the supply of commodities tends
to increase as more and more countries start to produce them
while demand grows only slowly in the developed countries.
And the way these commodities are sold, in an auction in
which the warehouse must be cleared whatever the level of
prices, contrasts with the way in which manufactured goods
are sold, the prices being fixed on a costs plus basis, with
the costs including an adequate standard of living for the
producers, consistently operates to the disadvantage of the
poorer countries (Elliott, 1987, 54–55). Similar problems occur
in domestic markets. A market system requires regulation to
protect the interests of the poor and prevent undue concentrations of wealth and power. If in the market you pay no
attention to the distribution of earnings, more needs to
be done through welfare to give people a tolerable level of
income. And this necessarily involves increased taxation.

(e) *Inflation*   To a significant extent inflation is caused by
failure to agree about the distribution of incomes, and in its
turn a high level of inflation has an adverse effect on income
distribution. Inflation in Britain has fallen to the lowest levels
it has known since the 1960s and has recently been running
at an annual rate of about 5%. This has been helped by falls
in world prices of oil, basic materials and foodstuffs and by
the availability of cheap imported consumer goods. Government policies have also contributed, both through the attempts
to restrict public spending and still more through the steep
rise in unemployment, which has reduced demand and
weakened the power of the unions in wage bargaining. But it
has also to be noted that inflation has a differential impact.
Poor people experience a higher level of inflation than the
more prosperous for a variety of reasons. The things they
have to spend more on, such as basic food, heating and

public transport, tend to rise in price faster than the average. And policies to control inflation also fall most heavily on the poor.

These, and other, mechanisms of distribution need to be synchronized if they are to be effective in tackling the stubborn problems of unfair distribution. And if the just distribution of wealth, incomes and benefits is seen as an important social priority, as it should be in our opinion, it must be accepted as an object of policy to be tackled directly.

8   *The global context*

If patterns and trends in distribution in Britain make us concerned and even angry, global inequalities can truly shock. In this section we outline some salient facts of global distribution to provide a context for our exploration of British inequalities.

(*a*) *Global inequality and poverty*   We turn first to inequalities between the incomes of the world's independent states. By dividing the total annual cash value of goods and services produced in a country by the population, we arrive at the annual income available to a person in that country – the per capita income, or pci. This calculation gives a measure of a country's material standards, but rides roughshod over internal inequalities within countries – a point to which we shall return later. None the less it gives a rough and ready indication of the standard of living in various countries.

The first column of figures in Table 3 gives the pci, in US\$ 1983, for selected countries, together with their rank order place out of 142. From pci figures, it is possible to calculate that the average pci for all countries defined as 'developed', with 24% of the world's population, is \$9417. The world's poorest sixteen countries, with 21.5% of the world population, have a pci averaging below \$240. This disparity would be greater if the populations were not grouped by countries: the presence of some wealthy people in the poorest countries, and of many poor people in the richest, softens the statistical extremes. Nevertheless, our figures suggest a

Table 3:   Gross National Product per capita, life expectancy, infant mortality rates and adult literacy rates for selected countries[1]

Country	1. GNP per capita US$ 1983	Rank	2. Life expectancy Years	Rank	3. Infant mortality Rate[2]	Rank	4. Literacy %[3]	Rank
Developed Countries	9417		73		17		99	
Developing Countries	736		59		90		60	
United States	14172	7	75	7	11	17	99	4
Brazil	2032	53	64	65	70	76	76	65
Ecuador	1319	68	63	70	70	76	82	59
Nicaragua	868	84	60	77	75	81	88	45
Peru	1064	77	59	82	86	84	84	55
Venezuela	4027	40	68	52	38	56	86	51
France	10481	16	75	7	9	9	99	4
W. Germany	11403	14	74	11	10	13	99	4
Netherlands	9869	20	76	4	8	5	99	4
Portugal	2270	51	71	33	19	33	82	59
Sweden	12444	9	77	1	7	4	99	4
United Kingdom	9171	22	73	21	10	13	99	4
Bulgaria	5897	32	72	26	17	31	95	31
E. Germany	7427	26	72	26	11	17	99	4
USSR	6784	28	70	44	31	48	99	4
Egypt	672	95	58	84	100	97	44	108
Saudi Arabia	12193	11	56	88	105	100	30	121
Syria	1675	65	66	58	55	68	56	93
Bangladesh	129	134	48	113	133	121	34	120
India	262	122	54	92	106	101	42	109
China	300	116	67	54	52	65	69	78
Indonesia	535	100	54	92	87	85	70	72
Japan	10154	19	77	1	6	1	99	4
Philippines	724	91	64	65	50	63	88	45
Australia	11514	13	75	7	10	13	99	4
Ethiopia	117	137	43	133	138	126	12	138
Kenya	347	110	56	88	63	70	52	98
Nigeria	734	90	50	103	130	119	38	111
Somalia	245	124	43	133	143	130	10	142
Burkina Faso	182	130	44	127	181	139	11	141
Zimbabwe	744	88	56	88	70	76	72	70

1. World rank order position out of 142 (= sign excluded). From Sivard, 1986, pp. 36–41. See Sivard, pp. 42–3 for notes on data, which in general refer to 1983
2. Rate of deaths under one year old per 1000 live births
3. % of population over 15 able to read and write

differential between the world's richest 20% and poorest 20% in excess of 40:1. A similar calculation for the richest and poorest fifths of the British population in 1976/7 gave a differential of just 7:1.

It is not easy to appreciate the standard of life endured by millions in the poorer countries. Other measures may give a fuller understanding of human realities. Columns 2–4 of Table 3 give figures for life expectancy, infant mortality and adult literacy which reveal alarming inequalities. An infant in Burkina Faso is more than 30 times as likely to die as one in Sweden or Japan. An Ethiopian or an Afghan can look forward, on average, to only 40 years of life – 35 years less than in most developed countries.

Various attempts have been made to arrive at some composite 'level of living' index for different countries. D.M. Smith compiled an index designed to comprise physical, mental and material well-being from six indicators (Smith, 1979, 70ff.). When plotted against national pcis, his figures suggest that while there is a clear relation between levels of personal income and the quality of life, there are diminishing returns in terms of improvements in the quality of life as income increases. Small increases in the incomes of poorer people produce greater benefits than small increases in the incomes of the wealthy (Smith, 1979, 73). Small transfers from the rich to the poor could add a great deal to the sum of human happiness!

Our figures not only indicate gross differences between the richer and the poorer countries; they pinpoint destitution. Destitute people are those who don't have enough for the basic necessities of life. In the late 1970s the World Bank estimated that 800 million people worldwide were destitute in this sense. Accepting this figure, the Brandt Commissioners interpreted it as 40% of the population of the countries of the 'South', excluding China (Brandt Commission, 1980, 50). Most of these destitute are found in rural areas in countries of the world's two most marked 'poverty belts' – that straddling sub-Saharan Africa and that encompassing major areas of South Asia. Many destitute are now also in urban areas, including the cities of Latin America. These urban poor endure the galling reality that their absolute poverty is lived alongside symbols of substantial wealth.

(b) *Internal inequality*   The extent of inequality within countries varies widely, especially where 'middle income' countries are concerned. In the poorest countries, the little income that exists is of necessity quite evenly distributed. As economic development proceeds, inequality tends to rise. The degree of inequality then appears to fall as we move to the world's richer countries with their more complex mechanisms for income redistribution.

The greatest inequalities seem to be exhibited by middle income countries, and in particular those controlled by a small elite group, perhaps racial or military in nature. This is the situation in many of the Latin American republics. Middle income countries can, however, curtail excessive inequality if they have the will to do so, as in the case of many such countries under Marxist control (Smith, 1979, 73; Ahluwalia, 1974, 3–37).

The world's wealthier countries – very roughly those with a pci above $2000 in 1986 – will be striving to achieve a universally applied pattern of social services, including such things as universal education and health care. To pay for such services, there will be a comprehensive taxation system which redistributes income. The extent of the redistribution will clearly depend on political and other factors, but in general it appears that the richer a country is the more radical will be its mechanism of redistribution. By world standards inequality in the UK is quite modest.

Indigenous wealth in Third World countries is likely to be concentrated in the cities, and it is to the cities that the rural poor flock in the hope and expectation of an improved life. The great cities of the less impoverished Third World countries thus provide the classic confrontations of inequality – squalid shantytowns cheek by jowl with air-conditioned luxury hotels. The inequalities are all the more poignant for being so visible.

(c) *Inequalitity reinforced* The extreme maldistribution of the world's resources is itself a moral outrage, but it is compounded by the way in which the North's wealth and the South's poverty are interlinked. The North controls the world's terms of trade through which prices are set, and the North also produces a massively dominant part of the world's investment capital. This means, among other things, that middle class investors in the developed countries derive benefit from production by the world's poor, and enjoy an advantage not so directly shared by poorer people in their own countries.

Multinational Companies (MNCs) constitute a significant mechanism for the transfer of wealth from South to North. No Scottish-based MNCs compare in size with the giant American companies, or even with larger European concerns. But it is notable that Scottish MNCs which do have major investments in the South find their activities there particularly profitable. For example, Coates Paton's South American operations in 1980 accounted for only 11.7% of turnover, but 29.1% of gross profits (Sinclair, 1982, 2).

Countries of the South are massively in debt to Northern financial institutions, and the problems of interest and capital repayment involved are serving to reinforce inequalities both between and within countries. The Brandt Report noted that in the three years 1979–81, the servicing of such debt would involve the transfer of $120 billion from South to North, a major distribution of wealth in favour of the rich (Brandt Commission, 1980, 223). The recycling of oil surpluses in the 1970s allowed Third World debt to grow very rapidly in the late 1970s. In the 1980s the terms of trade have deteriorated for primary producers, and interest rates have remained consistently high, largely because of American trade and fiscal policies. The debt burden has become impossible for many debtor countries. Total non-oil-exporting countries' debt rose from $280 billion in 1977 to $771 billion in 1984. Many major debtors had to approach the IMF for help by the end of 1982.

Help given has depended on the adoption by debtor nations of severely deflationary policies, the effect of which is felt most painfully by the poor. Internal inequalities are increased.

(*d*) *Trends* In 1970 the pci for all developed countries grouped together was 11.5 times as great as for all developing countries. By 1981 the populations of the developed countries were 10.8 times as well off as people in developing countries – hardly any change.

Even in the relatively favourable circumstances of the 1960s and 1970s, ten of the world's very poorest countries showed no improvement at all in pci. As a group, the world's 38 poorest countries achieved an annual growth rate of only 0.8% for pci in those two decades. Inequalities between countries of the South have been growing, and there is no evidence that the trend is being reversed.

Internally, growth in developing countries' economies has tended to accentuate inequalities. The Brazilian economy was one which grew fast during the 1960s. In 1970, the poorest 80% of the Brazilian population shared only 36.2% of the National Income, a reduction from the 45.5% of 1960. During the same period, the richest 1% of Brazilians increased their share of National Income from 11.7% to 17.8% (Duarte, 1979, 7).

(*e*) *Global redistribution* The inequalities within Britain described earlier in this chapter seem disturbing enough; yet Britain has various mechanisms for redistribution. There is no global system of redistribution in favour of the poor. Any benefit derived by the poor in the South as a result of Northern investment 'trickles down' as part of the productive process. It is not *re*distributed according to any canon of justice, let alone a bias to the poor.

The only significant mechanism of redistribution of income from rich to poor is aid. The total flow of official aid worldwide stood in 1980 at $38.9 billion. This can be compared with world military expenditure in the same year of $542.9 billion.

As a percentage of the GNP of donor countries in the

OECD's Development Assistance Committee, aid stood in 1980 at less than 0.4%. It had been that low since 1968. This contrasts with the United Nations target for aid of 0.7% of GNP. But the Brandt Report points out that even if its target of 1% were achieved it would not have a significant impact on the global distribution of wealth or income.

The only countries with a consistently good record as aid givers have been the Scandinavians, the Dutch, and some of the oil states. The British effort, which in 1979 was reaching 0.52% of GNP, is now down to 0.34%. No other area of government expenditure has been so severely cut in recent years.

Some people argue that overseas aid has a low political priority because it is not popular with the electorate. But the enthusiastic response to charitable appeals, most notably Bob Geldof's Band Aid, might lead one to question this. It is also relevant to point out that the countries with the best aid records – such as the Netherlands and the Scandinavian countries – have relatively even internal distributions of income and wealth. Would an internally fairer Britain be a fairer player at the international table?

The patterns and trends in global distribution are the British situation writ large. In both there is a steady increase in the number of the poor, ever broader gulfs between the poor and the rich, and great concentrations of wealth in a few hands. This all raises in stark and urgent form questions of justice and fairness. Maldistribution on this scale, and getting worse so fast, is socially disruptive and should not be tolerated in a decent society – in a nation like Britain, or in the 'global village'. We agree with the Anglican report, *Faith in the City* (1985) that 'Poverty is not only about shortage of money. It is about rights and relationships, about how people are treated and how they regard themselves; about powerlessness, exclusion and loss of dignity. Yet the lack of an adequate income is at its heart' (p. 195). But for the Christian great concentrations of wealth are also a moral problem. The creation of wealth should never be separated from the question of how to distribute resources in such a way as to strengthen fellowship and confirm human dignity. And Christians must have a special concern for the poor, who in Britain, as on the global scene, bear the brunt of hard times and recession, and do not benefit from prosperity as do others in our society.

We have seen in chapter one something of what maldistribution does to people and communities and why people who are not themselves poor but have encountered at first hand poverty and maldistribution have been challenged and changed. And now we have given some account of the processes and trends which have led to the present situation. We now turn to reflect theologically on what we have learned to see if we may discover some clues and hints as to the way forward.

Chapter Three

LOVE, JUSTICE AND SHARING: A CHRISTIAN PERSPECTIVE

1 Beliefs and attitudes

In earlier chapters of this book we have outlined facts and trends in distribution of wealth, income and benefits in Britain and around the world, and shown what this situation means for a variety of people. We have wanted the facts and the people to speak for themselves, and we have held back our own reactions and assessments. Readers will have found that some of the facts and trends have made them puzzled, concerned and even angry. In the Working Party, as we studied and discussed our material, we became profoundly disturbed about present trends in distribution. Our nation's failure to implement patterns of fair sharing has profound spiritual implications.

We found the facts challenging to many of our attitudes, beliefs and opinions. We hope that others also will allow their attitudes to be influenced by these facts. For all of us have some attitudes which have never been exposed to the facts, which are merely prejudices which ought to dissolve when we face reality, when we see how other people live, when we become aware of the human hopelessness and loss of dignity that poverty involves. Our attitudes are shaped significantly by our upbringing, by our education and social experience, by our material interests, by our ignorance or knowledge, and by our general view of the world. It is not only in South Africa or India that people, particularly prosperous people, can have no knowledge at all of how their fellows are living only a few miles away, and can deny that anything is wrong. It happens in Britain as well. It is easy to live in Bearsden and never visit Easterhouse, both within the same City of Glasgow, or to live in Morningside in Edinburgh and know nothing about Wester Hailes. And other cities in Britain all have their equivalents. Ignorance makes it easy to deny that a problem exists, and to reject responsibility for doing anything about it.

Attitudes are important. They reflect underlying beliefs. And they influence profoundly 'the way things go'. It was John Maynard Keynes, the economist, who wrote,

> I am sure that the power of vested interests is vastly exaggerated compared with the gradual encroachment of ideas. Not, indeed, immediately, but after a certain interval ... But, sooner or later, it is ideas, not vested interests, which are dangerous for good or evil (in Le Grand, 1982, 139).

Another economist, Julian Le Grand, ends a book in which he has shown how little progress there has been towards a fairer distribution of resources with an urgent call for a change in attitudes:

> To understand what people believe is crucial to understand the way they behave; and to change the way they behave, it is crucial to change what they believe. Indeed ideology can often override self-interest ... A change in beliefs can even induce people to reduce their power and privilege (Le Grand, 1982, 155).

But negative attitudes, even if they are no more than prejudices, can strengthen injustice and encourage the perpetuation of conditions which ought to be intolerable. Empirical studies such as Peter Golding and Sue Middleton's book, *Images of Welfare* (1982), have shown how common is the attitude of blaming the victim – the unemployed are work-shy, people on social security are 'the spoilt darlings and cheats of the welfare state' and so on. And other studies have shown that such attitudes are at least as common in the churches as outside. The more widespread such attitudes are the more likely it is that people will vote for repressive and uncaring policies, and fail to support moves towards more just distribution.

Christians should know that attitudes are important. Nor is it surprising that a great Christian social thinker, R.H. Tawney, believed that an 'intellectual conversion' was necessary if we were to have a juster and more Christian social order (Tawney, 1921, 223).

But Christians are also realists. They know that their interests and social position deeply influence their attitudes; they know that it is hard to 'bring every thought into captivity to Christ' (II Cor. 10.5).

In this chapter we invite the readers to set their attitudes about distribution alongside the Christian tradition, to share in our exploration of this tradition, and to use it as a kind of criterion of our opinions, and behaviour. We found this exploration a disturbing adventure, painful but enriching, the kind of continuous conversion, or constant checking of bearings and adjustment of route, that is an integral and unavoidable part of our pilgrimage.

And we think that this kind of exploration of the Christian tradition may also be useful for those who do not call themselves Christians. We live in an age when there seems to be no consensus about ultimate values, and fundamental disagreements about goals and objectives for society. Alastair McIntyre has argued that there is no longer an agreed criterion by reference to which the basic value conflicts of our day might be resolved (McIntyre, 1981). There is no doubt that we are in a state of considerable confusion about values and goals, and the way we should understand each other and our society. There is a new polarization between Right and Left, and dogmas and doctrines abound. Yet many find both poles unacceptable, and are profoundly confused and uncertain about the grounding of values, about the goals for social action, and about the kind of social relationships which are possible and desirable. We need to get back to fundamentals, and this involves looking once again at the insights of faith, at the religious tradition.

We do not claim to produce a 'Christian social theory',

or another set of dogmas, or a coherent system. Christian theology is just as much in crisis as any other intellectual project. Our aim is more modest. We invite the reader to explore with us the Christian tradition, particularly as it is found in the Bible, in the hope that we may find there clues, hints, and insights which may be helpful with our present problems, and challenging to some of the influential assumptions of our time. And we hope that our examination of the tradition may suggest some criteria relevant to the problems and dilemmas facing us today.

Questions of distribution – what is distributed, to whom, and in what way – are of importance to the Christian tradition because they raise major spiritual issues. As the Russian theologian, Berdyaev, said, bread for myself is a material matter, but bread for my neighbour is a spiritual matter. Any pattern of distribution expresses some understanding of the dignity and worth of the human individual, and must be measured against the Christian belief in the infinite value of each person and the equality of all before God.

A central theme of the Christian tradition is community. The only life worth living is life in fellowship, fellowship with God and with one's neighbours. Distribution, sharing, provides the sinews of community; loving involves sharing or it is not love. True community must express itself in patterns of distribution; distribution is for the sake of community. Fair or just distribution is integral to fellowship, the *koinonia* of which the New Testament speaks. Unfair distribution, great wealth and great poverty side by side, obstructs fellowship and splits communities into hostile or suspicious factions.

And some ways of distributing are demeaning and destructive; sharing that is grudging, or patronizing, or demands that the recipient shows himself to be 'deserving', humble and grateful, is fatally flawed from a Christian point of view. There is a difference between receiving something as a right, or as a gift, or as a reluctant charitable dole. Some modes of allocation create dependency, limit freedom and destroy dignity and self-respect; others encourage a proper balance

between independence and interdependence so that within
the community care and respect for one another flourish. At
the level of personal relations some patterns of distribution
are compatible with, or even encourage, loving relationships,
while other patterns impede or obstruct the growth of love.
For example, the relationship between a beggar and the
person from whom he solicits alms is so structured as to
make virtually impossible an authentic, caring relationship.
The passer-by is invited to give a paltry sum as a kind of
bribe to persuade the beggar to go away and terminate
the embarrassing relationship. There is no way within this
encounter of meeting the beggar's deeper needs, which are,
as with everyone, for care, respect, affection and a recognition of worth as well as for material resources. Neither
buying off the beggar with a couple of coins, nor refusing to
give alms, should ease the conscience of the passer-by. It is
the system which creates and tolerates such poverty, and the
parody of authentic caring relationships involved in beggary,
which are wrong. They offend against the conviction that
the beggar is the neighbour we have been given to love as
ourselves.

Christianity is centrally concerned with relationships and
with community. Our relationship to God and our relationship to our fellows are regarded as inseparable from one
another. Salvation understood as the healing of our relationship with God must show itself in renewed relationships
with our fellows. Healed – healthy – relationships must
express themselves in the way we share things, in patterns of
distribution. Distribution and community are inseparable
in the Christian tradition. Hence we can only discuss distribution in the context of community, fellowship, *koinonia*.

2 A sharing fellowship

(*a*) *The divine community* From the beginning, Christians
have found it necessary to think of God as more like a
community than an isolated person, a fellowship held together
by the closest and most intimate love and sharing. God's
own inner being is love. The God who loves us is love from

all eternity. God could not be God without being love; love is the essence of the divine community which Christians call the Holy Trinity – utterly reliable, constant, unchanging. There is no fickleness here, no arbitrary, unpredictable blowing hot and cold. In God, the Father, the Son and the Spirit are in perfect harmony, unity and diversity bound together by love and sharing, a model and source of what community might be and ought to be, fellowship without domination, love expressed in lavish sharing.

God's love 'spills over' upon his creation and particularly upon the women and men made to live in love with God and with one another. But human self-centredness has broken and denied love; human beings have become separated from God and from each other. Alienation, destruction and death are the inevitable consequences (Rom. 3.10–18). In Jesus Christ we see the definitive manifestation of the love of God, shown in his sharing of the human condition, entering into the fullest and most costly fellowship with human beings in all their lovelessness and need: God loved the world so much that he gave his only Son (John 3.16). In Jesus Christians believe God is at work restoring community and bringing the lost back into fellowship.

Jesus fulfilled his task by entering the human situation and plumbing its depths. He emptied himself, and took the nature of a slave (Phil. 2.7), that is, he shared in a special way with the poor, the alienated, the marginalized, and the rejected. His identification with people restored for them what they had lost – wholeness, health and dignity, hope and faith: life in its fullness, in fellowship with one another and with God. When he saw crowds of hungry people, harassed and helpless, let down by all those who should have been responsible for their welfare, he was 'moved with compassion' for them, because they were as sheep without a shepherd. The word commonly translated into English as 'moved with compassion' or 'filled with pity' is far stronger in the Greek. There it literally means 'to feel in the guts' – Jesus so shared the lot of the poor, hungry and powerless, of those who were manipulated by the leaders of society, of the despised and fearful, that he felt it as his own, he made their condition and destiny his.

In the gospel stories we see instance after instance illuminating the nature of God's love and showing how closely it is connected with sharing, with restoration of community, and with changes in people's attitudes and behaviour. Again and again we read how Jesus' behaviour surprised and shocked the religious, wealthy and influential people because he drew outcastes, prostitutes, sinners, cheats and all sorts of riff-raff into fellowship with himself, because he shared his table and his food, his time and his heart with people reckoned to be impure, with the marginalized, and with the excluded. He drew the lost and the bewildered with fellowship and shared himself with them. And in this sharing people were encountering the love and life of God. The feeding miracles were exemplary acts of distribution: 'You give them to eat', he said to his disciples (Matt. 14.16). And Jesus shared more than material resources with needy people – although the material food and drink were important both in themselves, as ways of meeting human need, and as signs of the bread of heaven and the water that slakes the thirst for ever. He shared himself, in countless convivial or costly ways, culminating in the cross. And the mode of Jesus' sharing deserves attention; he accepted people in all their diversity, he swept aside stigma to encounter the person within the label, he broke down social divisions and overcame ancient hostilities and suspicions.

Again and again in his teaching Jesus shows how bad distribution obstructs and destroys fellowship with God and with our fellows. In this life a great gulf has been created between the rich man and Lazarus, because the rich man in his luxury did not notice or respond to the needs of poor Lazarus lying at his gate. The gulf could have been bridged by the rich man reaching out to share his material resources with Lazarus as a sign of his love to the neighbour God had given him, and his obedience to the God of justice. But his failure in earthly, human fellowship results after death in an unbridgeable gulf between the rich man and Lazarus, their lots now reversed, and between the rich man and his God (Luke 16.19–31). The story of the Rich Young Ruler also shows in stark terms how wealth unshared obstructs fellowship: it is almost impossible (but with God all things are possible!) for a rich man to enter into the quality of loving, sharing relationships with God and with others which are characteristic of the Kingdom (Mark 10.17–31). The gospel of the Kingdom calls people to participate in the life of God, to enter into the fullness of community. And this participation involves sharing.

The costly reconciliation of the cross was the supreme act of community creation. The second chapter of the Letter to the Ephesians argues that through the blood of Christ those who were far off have been brought near, strangers have been brought into fellowship, and ancient dividing walls of hostility have been broken down. Suspicion and hostility have been brought to an end so that both Jews and Gentiles, and by implication all other antagonistic social groupings, are 'no longer strangers and sojourners, but fellow-citizens with the saints and members of the household of God' (Eph. 2.13–22). The Letter to the Hebrews speaks of Jesus on the cross bearing abuse outside the camp in solidarity with the rejected, the despised, and the marginalized. And believers are called to join him and them in fellowship there, and share his abuse (Hebrews 13.12–13). Finally, the resurrection of Jesus is God's affirmation that the new community cannot be destroyed and is valid for all.

(b) *Created community*   According to the Genesis creation narratives, and indeed the whole witness of scripture, God did not create human beings as isolated, self-sufficient entities, but as persons-in-relationship, in fellowship with God, with one another, and with the whole creation.

First, God created people in the context of the whole creation, which Calvin speaks of as 'the theatre of God's glory'. People are set as stewards, responsible to God for the flourishing of other creatures. Human stewardship excludes any idea of absolute ownership: God's gifts in the creation are to be used, enjoyed, cared for, and shared for the sake of community. Only God owns things in an absolute sense; he entrusts things to human beings to be used and distributed in accordance with his will, in fulfilment of his purposes of love. Throughout the Old Testament it is made clear that the creation is to be delighted in, and that material goods of all sorts, including land, are to be used responsibly to help the user and others, particularly the poor and weak, to flourish. Hoarding and accumulation by individuals in such a way that others are deprived of what they need is uniformly disapproved.

Secondly, God created human beings for fellowship: 'It is not good for the man to be alone' (Gen. 2.18). The image of God, it has been suggested, is reflected in the fellowship between woman and man (Gen. 1.27). In isolation a person is incomplete; only in fellowship, delighting in one another, loving one another, is God's creative purpose capable of fulfilment. And the central relationship is between God and the people God has made. The God-centredness of the creation is emphasized in the institution of the sabbath. According to the story, this is the day when God rested after the work of creation, and ever since it is a time set apart from the labour of life to enjoy the good creation, to delight in fellowship, and to remember that 'goods' are in fact gifts to us rather than the fruit of our efforts on which we have an absolute claim.

Thirdly, the creation story, and in particular the affirmation that people are made in the image of God, is a strong statement that the original and proper situation is one of equality. Everyone is of the same infinite value in the eyes of God. There is in the created order no hierarchy or ranking, no inferiority or superiority, no dominance or subordination. The kind of fellowship which is God's original and final purpose for human beings, the condition for true human flourishing, is that human beings should be treated as equally significant, equally important, equally entitled to love, equally capable of making a distinctive personal contribution to the enrichment of the community.

When Christians affirm the equality of all human beings they are asserting an equality of worth. Each and every individual is entitled to respect. This belief is rooted in the conviction that God has endowed each person with infinite worth as people created in his image. God in Christ gave himself for all equally, and the heart of Christian ethics is to love God and your neighbour as yourself. The neighbour is to be treated as an equal, with his needs and interests put on a par with one's own. This has clear distributional consequences. Absolute equality of resources is not demanded, but there must be such a redistribution as will allow human relationships to flourish. An insistence upon a more equal sharing of goods within the community is one important way in which we can recognize the status and claim of the other people God has given us to care for and love.

The story of the 'Fall' is a way of indicating that a fatal flaw has entered into the created order. People in fact amass belongings at the expense of others, use possessions to destroy fellowship and the justice on which community depends, and arrogantly claim absolute ownership, putting their trust in belongings and attempting to find their security in possessions. This attitude to possessions is denounced in the Bible as idolatry. The communal harmony of creation is disrupted by the lust for power, dominance and control. People become alienated from God and one another, estranged from the creation, which becomes a threat or a tool rather than a delight.

(c) *A pilgrim community*   An immensely influential model of what it means to be the People of God is rooted in the story of the journey out of bondage through the desert to the Promised Land. This motif is repeated again and again throughout the Bible, and is still today a powerful image of the kind of community that the church represents and offers to the world. 'The land flowing with milk and honey' is reached after the testing wilderness experience, but then a further goal lies ahead, and another, and another, until at last the final goal, 'the city, that has foundations, whose builder and maker is God' is attained (Heb. 11.10).

The pilgrim community does not settle down. The people are on the move towards a goal, and their whole life and activity can only be understood in the light of that goal. On the way, pilgrims discover what it is to be a community, a fellowship of aliens and exiles seeking their true home-land, and kept alive by hope. On the journey they learn to trust, support and understand one another; pilgrims depend on one another, and must have confidence in one another. Estranged and crippled fellowship becomes true community in the pedagogy of pilgrimage.

People on a journey travel light and must sit easy to possessions. It is absolutely necessary for people on the move to share. And the desert is not only a place of threat and danger, but above all a place of scarce resources, in which, the Exodus account is at pains to emphasise, God gives enough for all *provided* it is shared fairly. The stories of the manna – the bread from heaven – and the quails suggest that God provides for the needs of all, but not for greed. God's gifts are to be used, shared and enjoyed, not amassed or stored. The needs of each individual and family were met, so that there was neither scarcity nor waste. Hoarders are frustrated – 'He that gathered much had nothing over and he that gathered little had no lack' (Ex. 16.18). Accumulation is unnecessary and impossible – a kind of reminder that security lies in relationships with God and one's fellows rather than in amassing of possessions.

At the heart of the life of the pilgrim community is worship, the celebration of their relationship with God and with one another. God is with them, but is not a possession of the community. And yet the people again and again turn from God and from their goal, longing for the 'fleshpots of Egypt', the security of bondage, and abandoning the risky quest for the Promised Land. The height of their turning away from God was when, in Moses' absence, they took their jewelry and made a Golden Calf, a god, who was their possession, their plaything – the very epitome of the idolatry of material things, or riches. Here was mammon worship at its starkest and its most degrading, but also at its most obvious: then as now there were more subtle and unsuspected ways to worship material things and deny the living God who leads his people to their goal.

The pilgrim experience of the exodus, and others like it down the ages, is constantly referred to in the Jewish and Christian traditions as a definitive description of the life of faith and of the nature of the godly community. When God's people settle down they must never forget that 'A wandering Aramean was my father', that when they cried to the God of their fathers, 'the Lord heard our voice and saw our affliction, our toil and our oppression; and the Lord brought us out of Egypt with a mighty hand and an outstretched arm, with great terror, with signs and wonders; and he brought us into this place and gave us this land, a land flowing with milk and honey' (Deut. 26.7–9). Remembering this, the people are to offer firstfruits to God, to rejoice *with the strangers living among them* 'in all the good which the Lord your God has given to you and to your house' (v.11), and to share the fruits of the earth with the stranger, the fatherless and the widow – with those who still experience the reality of being exiles, who do not belong. The pilgrim experience of the past is constantly a reason for sharing, for just distribution, and for special care for the poor and the excluded. In the desert the Israelites discovered what it means to be the people of God, what true community is – and permanently valid principles of distribution.

(*d*) *Covenant community* In the covenant, God commits himself in steadfast love to the community, and calls on the people to respond as the 'beloved community' (to use Martin Luther King's evocative phrase). Jeremiah sums up the nature of the covenant thus: 'I will be your God and you shall be my people' (Jer. 7.23; 31.33). God's love is not offered on conditions, but those who are aware of being loved by God and bound to God in the loving covenant are enabled to respond and are shown how to respond to God and to one another within a fellowship of sisters and brothers.

Much of the Old Testament is concerned to indicate the kind of relationships which are proper in the beloved community.

These include many specific proposals for forms of distribution which may express the love and the justice of God and encourage fellowship among God's people. But there is also a realistic awareness that things go wrong, that over time some grow rich at the expense of others, that dominance and luxury and oppression reassert themselves even within the beloved community, perhaps as a sign that there is a flaw, a radical defect in the world as we know it, and in the way people behave. This is sin, which is often related to the story of the Fall (Gen. 3). Accordingly, mechanisms are necessary for bringing society back on course, for reasserting the patterns of distribution proper for the People of God, for reintegrating into the community the poor and the excluded.

One of these mechanisms was the Sabbatical Year, the holy seventh year when God's ordering of things was to be re-asserted (Ex. 23.10–11; Lev. 25.1–7; Deut. 15). The land was to lie fallow and rest, debts were to be cancelled and slaves must be released. The Sabbath Year had an ecological as well as a social dimension; it allowed the soil to recover, and it eased the pressure on the poor to repay borrowed money. The poor would also be able to reap whatever might grow wild on the land (Ex. 23.11). The argument for keeping the Sabbatical Year was twofold: first, Israel's own experience of poverty and slavery, and of the God who heard their cry and delivered them, should make them able to understand and deal generously with those who are poor and oppressed; and, secondly, in keeping the year, Israel will find blessing (Deut. 15.7–8, 10–11). Although it is questionable whether the Sabbatical Year was ever fully observed, it stands in the tradition as a constant reminder that regulatory mechanisms are necessary if human selfishness is to be curbed and a fair pattern of distribution with special provisions for the weak and the poor maintained.

The legislation for the Jubilee Year, occurring every fifty years, was along the same lines, but more radical (Lev. 25.8–55). As it was designed to coincide with a Sabbatical Year, the same rules applied. In addition, however, there was to be a return to the original distribution of land: since all land belongs to God, humans can have no absolute ownership, and possession of land can only be temporary. Since the land was a gift of God to his pilgrim people, the original pattern of distribution which gave each tribe and family its fair allocation of land had to be restored regularly. 'The land shall not be sold in perpetuity, for the land is mine; for you are strangers and sojourners with me' (Lev. 25.23).

Special provisions in the law protected the interests of widows, orphans, the poor, and strangers who did not belong to the community. They were to be dealt with generously, allowed to glean the harvest fields, and provided with the necessities of life. When Israel had been poor and defenceless they had met a God who cared for them gently, liberated them from bondage, and provided for their needs. In prosperity Israel must never forget to share in God's special concern for the poor and vulnerable. And such matters could not be left to individual, spontaneous charity; because of the acquisitiveness and selfishness of human beings, even God's people, they must be the subjects of law. This law declares God's will for just sharing, for fair distribution. The legislation is not against property as such, although it does constantly suggest that we are no more than temporary stewards for our property, but it seeks to prevent luxury and 'conspicuous consumption' on the one hand and poverty on the other. These things offend God, destroy community, and degrade people.

Again and again economic practices in Israel contradicted the justice of God. The prophets protested, defending the community and in particular the weak and poor against those who would deny the covenant and rebel against the justice of Jahweh. Sometimes the prophets denounce individual behaviour, as in Nathan's parable about the rich man who stole from the poor man the one lamb that he had in order to entertain his guest (II Sam. 12.1–6).

But with the great prophets, particularly Hosea, Amos, Micah and Isaiah, criticism increasingly turns against *systems* of oppression, as they denounce a society which they perceive to be corrupt and in rebellion against God's justice, because it is dominated by those 'who oppress the poor, who crush the needy' (Amos 4.1). Poverty was understood as the result of oppression and injustice, and God accordingly stands to judge his people: '"What do you mean by crushing my people, by grinding the face of the poor?" says the Lord God of hosts' (Isa. 3.13–15). And

> Woe to those who decree iniquitous decrees, and the writers who keep writing oppression, to turn aside the needy from justice and to rob the poor of my people of their right, that widows may be their spoil, and that they may make the fatherless their prey! What will you do on the day of punishment, in the storm that will come from afar? To whom will you flee for help, and where will you leave your wealth? (Isa. 10.1–3).

The question at issue is not almsgiving, what is today called 'charity', but *restitution* to the poor of what is properly theirs, *restoration* of God's just pattern of distribution. The true service of God involves the doing of justice; without it worship becomes hateful to God:

> I hate, I despise your feasts, and I take no delight in your solemn assemblies. Even though you offer me your burnt offerings and your cereal offerings, I will not accept them, and the peace offerings of your fatted beasts I will not look upon. Take away from me the noise of your songs; to the melody of your harps I will not listen. But let justice roll down like waters, and righteousness like an ever-flowing stream (Amos 5.21–24).

What the Lord requires of his people is 'to do justice, and to love kindness, and to walk humbly with your God' (Micah 6.8). Oppression of the poor and denial of just distribution make authentic worship and a proper relationship to God impossible. It is a denial of the covenant relationship with Jahweh (Epsztein, 1986).

Finally, there is in the Old Testament a vision that just distribution will be restored (Ez. 47.13f.). Special consideration is to be given to the aliens in Israel; they too are to have fair shares and to be treated 'as native-born sons of Israel'. Everyone is to enjoy just distribution in the new community. In the great vision of the future in Isaiah 65, God proclaims that he is creating a new heaven and a new earth, that there will be a life without suffering and distress. The situation which had been attacked by the prophets will be reversed, the dispossessed will have their own houses and fields, and the exploited will enjoy the fruit of their labour. Here is hope for the poor and the oppressed.

(e) *A new community* The old covenant was always in danger of becoming a legal and external affair, and God's people often found ways of avoiding the kind of relationships which the covenant called for. Thus there was the hope for a new covenant, a covenant in the heart, an internalization of the love and justice embodied in God's covenant, expressed joyfully and spontaneously in lifestyle and in sharing. The Lord who loves justice will make an everlasting covenant with his people (Isa. 61.8), writing his law upon their hearts (Jer. 31.33).

This new covenant was inaugurated, Christians believe, when Jesus, sharing a meal with his disciples, took the cup and said, 'This cup is the new covenant in my blood', signifying his death on the cross the following day. The new covenant community is in principle inclusive. At its centre is sharing, in the eucharistic feast, in the dying and rising of its Lord, in sharing of material things, and of hopes and fears.

The new community starts with the little group of disciples called by Jesus to share in his mission and be with him. From that point it expands to include ever wider circles of people of immense diversity. The call of Jesus into fellowship challenges and renews people in all dimensions of their lives. It is a call into community and away from all forms of self-centredness, and in particular from putting one's trust in material riches since 'your heart will always be where your riches are' (Matt. 6.21). No one can serve two masters, God and mammon (Matt. 6.24) (Johnson, 1986). Instead, Jesus invites his followers to enter into a caring, sharing fellowship with each other and with the broader community. In the feeding miracles, where the narratives include echoes of the manna stories and are anticipations of the joyful sharing that will take place in the coming messianic banquet, the disciples are given an active role in ensuring fair distribution: 'You give them to eat', Jesus told them (Mark 6.37). The life of the new covenant community is expressed in the sharing rather than in the having; those who give reap great rewards, while hoarders find that their treasure disintegrates.

A favourite image of the church in Paul's writings is the body; all members are dependent on Christ the head and on each other. There is no Christian life in isolation. In the first century, a time of considerable economic strain for the poor in Palestine, the Christian congregations tried to live as communities so that God's love should shine through the way they led their common life. Christians share in Christ and in his benefits, and this is inseparable from sharing material resources.

The accounts of the life of the Jerusalem church in Acts 2 and 4 suggest that distribution was in terms of need, not status or previous wealth. But the Jerusalem church was a poor church, and Paul arranged a collection among the Gentile churches to assist them (II Cor. 8 and 9, Gal. 2.10, Rom. 15.26ff., Acts 11.27–30). This aid should be motivated by love, and by the spiritual example of Jesus himself, who 'though he was rich, yet for our sake he became poor, so that by his poverty you might become rich' (II Cor. 8.9). In assisting the Jerusalem church materially, the Corinthian church is repaying a spiritual debt, acting in a Christlike way, and maintaining fellowship (*koinonia*) between the churches. This 'cheerful giving' glorifies God, and makes the giver richer, not poorer, because in it is experienced the love of Jesus and the riches of fellowship.

'By this all men will know that you are my disciples, if you have love for one another' (John 13.35). Love is the sign that they are God's children (I John 4.7) and the demonstration that the church is indeed the family of God, the household of faith. This image of the church as the loving family of God is the basis for the repeated injunctions of the Johannine epistles, 'Little children, love one another'. Love for the sisters and brothers is an essential part of what it means to be a Christian and a member of the fellowship called the church. Faith must become active in love or it is not faith; without love the knowledge and service of God is impossible, for God *is* love. Love is the necessary expression of faith.

Loving is thus a way of participating in the being of God: 'Beloved, let us love one another; for love is of God, and he who loves is born of God and knows God. He who does not love does not know God; for God is love' (I John 4.7–8). In loving we come to know God, whether we recognize intellectually what is happening or not. This love is shaped by and reflects the love of God, the love which God is. It is generous, self-giving, ungrudging; it has all the qualities so magnificently celebrated in the great hymn of love in I Corinthians 13: 'So faith, hope and love abide, these three; but the greatest of these is love.'

God's love is expressed most fully in the sending of Jesus Christ, in his life, teaching, relations, death and rising. In him we see what love really is; he is love made manifest. But there is more at issue here than the provision of a model, an instance, the supreme example of love. If that were all that God offers us it would expose our incapacity for loving, our lovelessness and self-absorption and leave us guilty, discontented and forlorn. But God loves us in our lovelessness and unlovableness, God accepts us as we are, without qualification or demand.

My song is love unknown,
My Saviour's love to me,
Love to the loveless shown, that they might lovely be.
O who am I, that for my sake
My Lord should take frail flesh and die? (Samuel Crossman)

By being loved we discover what love is, and only thus are we set free to love.

The church, then, is the fellowship of those who *know* that they have been loved by God, by the God who loves and cares for all whether they know this or not. Those who know that they have been accepted and loved by God despite everything are set free to love others, especially those who have no claim on their affection, those who are tied to them by no natural bonds of relationship. No one, to the beloved of God, is unlovable.

'Look how these Christians love one another' ought to be said more often than it is, for the love of Christians should be the confirmation of the gospel which they preach and the faith they celebrate. Love among believers, love within the church, is more than a desirable characteristic of a particular religious community: without this crucial quality in relationships, the Christian fellowship cannot be the sign and provisional manifestation of the coming Kingdom. Love among Christians should point to the Kingdom of love and peace, and attract others into the service of that Kingdom. It should be a light to guide the nations on their way, a persistent challenge to the lovelessness of the world, and a beacon of hope to those who despair of ever finding love.

3 Love and justice

Love and justice are very closely related in the Bible and the Christian tradition, but they are not in fact the same; there are subtle and important differences of emphasis. One may say that love is the inwardness of justice, the clue to the real meaning of justice. Doing justice then becomes a way of loving, indeed the only way of loving that is possible when large numbers of people are in question and when we are dealing with groups and collectivities. Justice can be spoken of as love distributed, the way in which a community loves its members. 'Love at a distance' it has been called.

Or justice may be seen as providing the necessary conditions for loving, as enabling love. Even in the most loving of families children constantly complain about unfairness, real or imagined, in the distribution of sweets or the time for going to bed. Such protests should be understood as a kind of testing of the value structure of the family against the universal assumption that distribution should be fair. Persistent injustice-as-unfairness in a family, or in any other community for that matter, is an effective sign of the death of love, and is itself destructive of fellowship.

The close relationship between love and justice not only means that the two are mutually supportive so that you cannot have one without the other, but also that we should expect each to flavour the other. Justice should be done in a loving fashion. God's justice and God's mercy belong together, and human justice, like God's, should be committed especially to the vindication of the poor and mercy for the oppressed. The justice of the Bible must not be thought of as a mere distributive arrangement, allocating goods of various sorts among people and groups. The manner in which justice is done, the attitude and motivation matter.

Love in its Latin garb as 'charity' has been devalued in modern usage by frequently being separated from justice so that it becomes grudging hand-outs to the 'deserving poor' rather than giving a person that person's due. Such patronizing charity degrades the recipient and salves, but does not challenge, the conscience of the giver. It has little if anything to do with love interpreted in the light of justice, or with justice seen as inseparable from love. Properly understood, we cannot conceive of love and justice as being at war with one another; rather we correct and strengthen our practice of each in the light of the other. Love without justice is in danger of becoming sentimental and irrelevant; justice without love easily becomes judgmental and uncaring.

It would be radically misleading to suggest that in the Old Testament we encounter a God of justice, while the God of the New Testament is a God of love. The Book of the Prophet Hosea is only the most sustained of many discussions of the love of God in the Old Testament. And the New Testament does not forget that the God who is love cares passionately for justice. The liberation theologian Jôsé P. Miranda argues very convincingly that in the Old Testament knowing God and doing justice, serving God and doing justice are the same thing (Miranda, 1977, 35–72). Knowing God is identified with the practice of justice and righteousness and the defence of the poor and needy (Jer. 22.15–16). The service which God desires is not sacrifices and holocausts, not cultic, religious activity, but justice: 'For I desire steadfast love and not sacrifice, the knowledge of God rather than burnt offerings' (Hos. 6.6. Cf. Hos. 8.13, Amos 5.21–25, Isa. 1.11–17, Micah 6.6–8, Jer. 6.18–21, 7.4–7, 11–15, 21–22, Isa. 43.23–24, 58.2, 6–10, etc.). And the doing of justice, Miranda argues, is understood as loving the poor and meeting their needs, by this redistribution moving towards a restoration of God's design for human life in fellowship.

Establishing just social structures and doing justice are no simple matters. Our interests and our sinfulness distort our view of justice. It is particularly hard for individuals or groups to see that justice may demand that they give up something, that they may be worse off materially than before. Prosperous and powerful groups usually believe that the status quo is just, and defend their privilege in the name of justice. Society is full of conflicts of interest, and the establishment of justice is rarely possible without conflict. Christians who believe that God has a special care for the poor and weak must school themselves to rise above their own interests in order to seek God's justice. And doing justice can involve taking sides in conflicts in a world that is full of injustice and lovelessness.

Doing justice and loving are, in both Old and New Testaments, complementary descriptions of the same kind of behaviour. The God of love and justice calls people to a specific practice in relation to their material goods as an expression of their fundamental attitude to God and their fellows: 'If anyone has the world's goods and sees his brother in need, yet closes his heart against him, how does God's love abide in him? Little children, let us not love in word or speech but in deed and in truth' (I John 3.17–18). Justice is the way the beloved community structures its life.

As the old marriage service recognized ('all my worldly goods with thee I share'), loving involves a glad, generous sharing of material possessions. The sharing is an expression of the loving. It is not a precondition for love; someone who said, 'I will love you in return for a third of your income', would in fact be denying rather than affirming love. The sharing follows naturally, spontaneously from the loving. And similarly an eagerness to share, and to share in ways which enhance and do not demean the recipient, should be a natural outcome of encountering the God of justice and of love. The justice and the love of God should be reflected in fair sharing among God's children. Fair sharing encourages love and community; unfair distribution is disruptive of fellowship.

4   *The needs of neighbours*

(a) *Neighbours and strangers*   The dictionaries give as the primary meaning of 'neighbour', 'a person who dwells near another', and etymologically the word goes back to a Germanic root meaning 'near-farmer'. A neighbour is someone who lives near one, in the same neighbourhood; someone who is almost certainly very like oneself, since birds of a feather flock together. In an Indian village the people who used to be called Untouchables live apart from the main village in their own *cheri*, and do not use the same wells or the common facilities of the village. They are different, they are not neighbours; the caste people feel that they may treat them in a quite different way from their own kind, their neighbours. Slaves and servants, even if they lived in the master's house, were seldom if ever regarded as neighbours; they did not belong, they were different, they might support the life of the neighbourhood – without their work it would be impossible – but they were not part of it.

Townships and shantytowns around South African cities demonstrate the same point: those who live in Soweto may work in Johannesburg, but they do not belong there, they are not neighbours to those who live in the city, who for the most part know little of the life of people in Soweto. Nor is it much different with us. Our cities are surrounded with peripheral housing estates which are alien worlds to most people in the middle-class residential areas. Our society is full of policies and structures which obstruct the development of neighbourliness by encouraging ignorance of how other people live.

Neighbours in the basic sense belong to a face-to-face community; they know one another. Neighbours may squabble, but they tend to stand shoulder-to-shoulder against any outside threat or challenge. And neighbours often care for one another in warm and wonderful ways – the woman in a tenement stair, for instance, who gives her elderly neighbour a daily cup of soup and unobtrusively checks that everything is all right. There are recognized standards of good neighbourliness which everyone knows, even if we often fail to live up to them. Neighbours have responsibilities to one another – that is an assumption in every society, a basic part of natural morality which does not require to be validated by religion. Neighbours belong together; they are interdependent; they ought to be able to rely on one another.

When the Bible enjoins us to love our neighbour, or to do justice to our neighbour (as in the Ten Commandments, Ex. 20.16–17/Deut. 5.20–21), it is often this natural neighbour who is in question. But already in the Old Testament there is a significant extension of the meaning of the neighbour. In Leviticus 19.18, for instance, there is an injunction to love the neighbour, and the context makes abundantly clear that the neighbour is the brother, the son of your own people. But towards the end of the same chapter (vv. 33–34) the Israelites are exhorted to love the strangers in their midst: the marginalized people are to be loved and accepted as if they were themselves physical neighbours; the excluded people are to be incorporated into the moral community of Israel and treated as neighbours. The contrast with the treatment of slaves and *metoikoi*, resident aliens, in the cities of the ancient world, and 'guest-workers' and ethnic minorities in many modern societies could hardly be more stark. The stranger is to be treated as a neighbour, the Old Testament suggests, for two specific reasons: the Israelite memory of having been themselves strangers in Egypt should have taught them the bitterness of exclusion and made them sensitive to the pain of others; and, secondly, again and again they had found that their God, the God of Israel, was a God who has a special care for strangers, the despised, the poor and the oppressed.

In the parable of the Good Samaritan (Luke 10.25–37), it is the stranger, the despised and hated foreigner, the heretic excluded from the covenant people, the feared Samaritan who shows himself through his actions to be the neighbour of the Jew, lying wounded and forlorn by the roadside. The stranger acts graciously as a neighbour to his fellow who needs his help. The alien becomes the neighbour. This earth-shaking assertion that the stranger and the enemy are neighbours, that strangers are neighbours, that people quite different from us are our neighbours, that people we do not know are our neighbours, vastly expands the sphere of moral responsibility.

(b) *The neighbour's needs* All these people are to be loved! And all may offer us love in our need and lovelessness, as did the Good Samaritan! On the one hand, we are taught that love to God and love to the neighbour thus understood are inseparably linked together (Matt. 5.43–46). And on the other hand, you are to love your neighbour as yourself; that is, you are to treat the neighbour's interests like your own, the neighbour's needs are to be taken at least as seriously as your own, and you are to be fair, generous and compassionate to your neighbour. And this kind of love necessarily involves the sharing of material things in a loving way.

My neighbour is a particular person with quite specific claims on me and a distinctive contribution to make to the good of others. The neighbour is not to be assessed in terms of income, wealth, status, or achievement. The Samaritan was of infinite worth to the Jew lying wounded beside the Jericho road, because he acted as a neighbour to him, because he fulfilled his obvious and clamant needs. And in a rather different way the Samaritan needed the Jew, needed to help him, and thereby affirmed his worth, so cruelly denied by the thieves. The human dignity of Jew and Samaritan, transcending their differences, was affirmed in and by the establishment of a neighbourly relationship, in the recognition that they were neighbours, who needed one another.

Several attempts have been made in recent times to develop an understanding of human nature in terms of needs. The psychologist Mallman, for instance, sees human needs as finite and constant over time, while the satisfiers are extremely varied and culturally determined. Other thinkers such as Maslow make similar attempts to explain what it is to be human, what we share beneath our differences, in terms of needs. Maslow produces a hierarchy of needs – some are more important than others. No one suggests that all needs are material. Freedom, love, identity, a sense of meaning, to name just the most obvious ones in Mallman's list, go far beyond basic biological requirements.

Needs seem to divide into two categories; there are biological needs which require to be met if life is to be sustained, and there are social and spiritual needs which should be satisfied if human beings are to flourish. There is more or less general agreement about the needs that go into the first category, but it is by no means as clear what human flourishing is, or what needs must be met if human beings are to flourish. Michael Ignatieff argues that 'a decent and humane society requires a shared language of the good' (Ignatieff, 1984, 14), but it is precisely this that we lack today. And by default we either leave it to politicians and bureaucrats to decide what people's needs are, what is good for them, and by implication what human flourishing is, or we take people's *wants* as defining their *needs*. This allows the poor's envy of the rich and the rich's pride of possession to corrupt our understanding of human flourishing by making it a purely material matter. People need more than the fulfilment of their material needs; but material needs are important none the less.

The need of the neighbour is a principle of distribution of the first importance. The neighbour's needs, the Christian faith teaches, should be taken as seriously as my own. The neighbour has a claim on me, and often I must delay or deny the satisfaction of my own needs if I am to meet the needs of my neighbour. The needy neighbour must be helped in proportion to his need; status, qualities, achievements, membership of the church, are all irrelevant at the point of need. Needs must be met. 'When we give out food, we will attend directly to the purpose of the giving: the relief of hunger. Hungry men and women don't have to stage a performance, or pass an exam, or win an election' (Walzer, 1983, 75). That is why the old and persistent distinction between the 'deserving' and the 'undeserving' poor is so vicious and pagan.

In the story of the sheep and the goats in Matthew's gospel, chapter 25, it is those who have responded directly and generously to the needs of the neighbour without realizing that in doing so they are in fact fulfilling the needs of Christ who are accepted. Only those who attend to the neighbour's need – which may well be different from the neighbour's wants – without thought of earning merit, or justifying themselves, or salving their consciences, are taking the neighbour with due seriousness and treating him with respect. For the manner in which needs are met and things are distributed matters, and matters profoundly. A need may be met in a way which demeans and humiliates the recipient, which in practice denies that he is a neighbour – or in a manner which enhances dignity and self-respect. Only the latter draws people into fellowship, strengthens their sense of meaning and significance, and sustains community.

The needs of neighbours are met by societies and communities as well as by individuals. In Matthew 25 it is the nations, not individuals, who are called to account for the extent to which they have met the needs of people. Only a society which recognizes this responsibility for the corporate meeting of needs can be a moral society. A society which recognizes need as a principle of distribution must ensure that the indirect exchanges between strangers mediated by the institutions of the society protect the dignity of both parties to the exchange. Ignatieff argues that the welfare state provides just such a structure of moral relations between neighbours who remain strangers to one another:

[Poor people] have needs, and because they live within a welfare state, these needs confer entitlements – rights – to the resources of people like me. Their needs and their entitlements establish a silent relationship between us. As we stand together in line at the post office, while they cash their pension cheques, some tiny portion of my income is transferred into their pockets through the numberless capillaries of the state. The mediated quality of our relationship seems necessary to both of us. They are dependent on the state, not upon me, and we are both glad of it. Yet I am also aware of how this mediation walls us off from one another. We are responsible for each other, but we are not responsible to each other (Ignatieff, 1984, 9–10).

It is, of course, possible to confuse a serious engagement with the language of needs with a glib and superficial longing for the instant satisfaction of every human want and desire. This is the ethos of the consumer society, which Tony Walter attacks so vigorously in his *All You Love is Need* (Walter, 1985). Christians above all must resist being dragged into a fashionably restricted understanding of human needs and human flourishing. Human beings, neighbours, need more than a fair distribution of material things, more than a human manner of meeting needs – they need a sense of meaning, a destiny, a purpose.

There are needs that neither politics nor a friendly neighbour may fulfil. Michael Ignatieff laments that in a secular age we have forgotten the language of transcendence, that we no longer speak of ultimate consolation and explanation: 'We can no longer offer each other the possibility of metaphysical belonging: a shared place, sustained by faith, in a divine universe. All our belonging now is social' (Ignatieff, 1984, 78). But this is just the possibility that the Christian gospel continues to hold out, the fundamental need the fulfilment of which it promises.

(c) *The need for neighbours* The needs of neighbours have a claim both upon individuals and upon society. Among the needs of all of us is the ability to fulfil others' needs. We should recognize that there is a mutuality in need, that we need one another and God, that we need fellowship, we need to participate. We need both to care and to be cared for. The needs of neighbours have a claim on us, and we need neighbours. We must learn to share need with our neighbours; there is a solidarity of need.

This point was made very strongly by Karl Barth in his notable discussion of the parable of the Good Samaritan (Barth, 1956, 411–52). The lawyer who, 'seeking to justify himself', asks Jesus, 'Who is my neighbour?' is the religious expert. He knows the law, he quotes the double commandment to love God and neighbour. His question, 'And who is my neighbour?' comes as a response to Jesus' words: 'You have answered right; do this, and you will live.' It betrays a fundamentally mistaken attitude to his fellows, and to God as well. If he does not know who his neighbour is, he cannot love him. He does not ask who God is. He thinks he knows the answer! But it is impossible for one who does not know and love his neighbour to know and love God. The lawyer's efforts to justify himself are really incompatible with love to God or neighbour, for he is subordinating their claims to his own, trying to use them for his personal justification, not taking them seriously in their own right. One might expect the lawyer to be guided by the parable to see in the Jew lying wounded by the roadside the opportunity given to him, the lawyer, in his strength, to do good to his neighbour. Here was an opportunity to fulfil the commandment to love the neighbour. But instead the story invites the lawyer to see himself as lying by the roadside, vulnerable and without resources, the recipient of compassion from the alien, the stranger, 'who makes no claim at all but is simply helpful'. Only so could the lawyer have been set free from self-righteousness, set free to accept God's compassion. And in recognizing his own need for a neighbour he would have been enabled in his turn to love God and his neighbour.

In his need my neighbour does me good. We need neighbours and we need to serve neighbours if we are to have a proper understanding of ourselves – and (far more important) if we are to serve and know Christ, whether we recognize him in the neighbour or not. The reciprocal ties of neighbourly fellowship create community and point beyond themselves to the fulfilment of fellowship in God.

(d) *The neighbour as citizen* The needs of my neighbour create obligations for me; or to put the matter the other way round, on account of his needs my neighbour has an entitlement to some of my resources and responses. The neighbour, in other words, has rights which both I and society should recognize and implement.

Needs and rights are not alternative terms for the same thing. People need love, belonging, dignity, forgiveness and understanding, but it hardly makes sense to speak of 'rights' to such intangible but essential goods. These things have more to do with gift and grace than with debt and obligation. People have rights to a fair trial, to welfare, to the vote, to a minimum income, and so forth. Needs may be met in such a way as to emphasise that the recipients are not wholly part of the community, to stigmatize and exclude them. Needs-as-rights can only be met by the recognition that the recipient as a full member of the community is entitled to receive them.

Citizenship, to use the most apt term for community membership, involves duties or responsibilities as well as rights. The citizen contributes to, as well as receiving from, the community of which he is a member. The citizen works, and votes, and pays taxes as well as receiving medical care and an old age pension. But the reciprocity of rights and duties does not mean that one's rights are *in proportion to* one's contribution. A decent community recognizes that it has a responsibility for the welfare of those – the severely handicapped, for example – who cannot make a major contribution of the usual sort to the wealth and prosperity of the community. In doing so, the community recognizes their dignity as human beings and their rights as full citizens, full members of the community.

When we say that citizenship involves rights and duties, we do not imply that the community creates rights, that it is free to award them, or take them away at will. Christians believe that ultimately rights are conferred by God as a way of affirming human dignity as creatures made in the image of God. Society ought increasingly to recognize and implement these rights. Such recognition of human rights must be, to some extent, redistributive, and should serve to reinforce and enrich the sense of membership in the community – in one word, citizenship.

In modern times, and especially since the Beveridge reforms in the 1940s, it has become widely accepted that as a matter of right citizens in Britain are entitled to an income adequate to maintain a decent standard of life, to health care of quality, to good education, and to welfare provision in times of hardship. In a Christian country this should surely have been accepted all along. As the Breadline Britain survey for London Weekend Television has shown, there is now a remarkable consensus in Britain today on the necessities regarded as necessary for a proper style of life (Mack and Lansley, 1985).

Marshall concentrated on the provision of welfare and other social rights by the state, and said nothing about the relation of the private provision of welfare to the concept of citizenship (Marshall, 1950). Much welfare is provided in relation to status as an employee rather than as a citizen. Whereas most state welfare is universal, and egalitarian in the sense that it is provided in principle (if not always in practice) to each citizen in relation to need rather than status or income, private welfare reflects and strengthens class inequality and makes for increased social differentiation.

At times the Exchequer subsidy to the occupational pensions of half of the working population has exceeded the Exchequer subsidy to the state pension scheme which covers the majority – while some 18% of state pensioners still require a means-tested supplementary pension in order to avoid severe poverty. The principle at work here seems to be the very opposite of a bias to the poor; it is the state ensuring that the prosperous stay rich while the poor remain in their poverty. We believe that welfare benefits should be regarded as rights of citizenship and financed by progressive taxation paid by those in work. As Richard Titmuss argued in the 1960s, what we refer to as benefits are often not benefits at all. Rather than being *additions* to the welfare of individuals, they are in effect *compensation* for the inevitable diswelfares involved in industrial and social change. Change brings gains for some and losses – most notably unemployment – for others. It should be a responsibility of citizenship, as it is of neighbourliness, to try to compensate fellow citizens for the costs they bear as a consequence of the benefits others enjoy.

Rights are important in themselves, but they are also means of social integration and ways of expressing the worth of the individual when they combine in the concept of citizenship. Citizenship fosters and embodies important attitudes, social relationships, styles of behaviour and understandings of the nature of human beings. An adequate level of material well-being by way of social rights, participation in the exercise of power in the community through political rights, and individual freedom and justice through civil rights are all desirable because of the kind of people they enable citizens to be. Such rights encourage more neighbourly relations within a less divided community, they enable people to be treated with a proper dignity, and they protect the ability of all, but particularly the poor and the weak, to participate in the life of the community.

People need one another, they need love, fellowship, community, they are interdependent. Nor should they be at the mercy of others who are more powerful and wealthy and can therefore manipulate and use them. Love draws the neighbour out of isolation and into fellowship, while protecting the neighbour's individuality. Thus we recognize the status and the claim of the neighbour God has given us.

5 A living tradition

We have discussed the foundations of a tradition of concern with issues of distribution, asking whether we can find there clues or hints which may be helpful in our present perplexities. Like all traditions, this one changed and developed down the centuries, as attempts were made to apply Christian insights in different circumstances and social contexts. Ideas developed in a simple nomadic or pastoral society are not easy to apply directly in a complex modern industrial society. But none the less the insights developed in the Judaeo-Christian tradition are profound and important. Christians all down the ages have felt that they are of perennial relevance, and that it is important to see how best they may be expressed in each age and society. We stand in a remarkable continuity of concern with distribution; Christians today are stewards of a living heritage.

It is a tradition of *protests* against unfair, demeaning and socially divisive distribution; of attempts at *regulation* of the economy to ensure a greater degree of justice in the way things are distributed; of the development of various *alternative forms of community life* in which sharing in distinctively Christian ways is integral to fellowship with God and one's fellows. And the Christian church has sometimes seen itself as such an alternative community, with each congregation showing at the local level a way of sharing. Thus we end the chapter with a short study of how the Church of Scotland distributes its own resources.

(a) *Protests* As the church grew more wealthy, as it became more 'established', and as the prosperous classes became Christian, protests against luxury, against inequality, against great wealth alongside great poverty continued and in some ways became more sharp. The Fathers sound very like the Old Testament prophets. A whole succession of popular protest movements appealed to the Bible for support. Christianity regularly fuelled the search for more just and equal distribution, attended to complaints from the victims of maldistribution, and sparked off protests.

The economic teaching of the gospels was very radical. The earliest Christian writers tried to be faithful to this teaching in a culture in which attitudes to wealth and poverty were sometimes diametrically opposed to Christian notions. They were, of course, influenced by their context, and sometimes borrowed economic ideas from pagan philosophy. But what was most remarkable was that in their teaching and in their attempts to be relevant to their own society's problems they maintained a strong tone of Christian radicalism.

Clement of Alexandria (c. 150–216) was a theologian who sought a kind of synthesis of Christian wisdom and classical scholarship; he was deeply influenced by Stoicism. But he taught that property was only justifiable for the sake of fellowship:

It is God himself who has brought our race to a *koinonia* by sharing himself, first of all, and by sending his Word (Logos) to all alike, and by making all things for all. Therefore everything is common, and the rich should not grasp a greater share (Avila, 1983, 37).

God's gracious provision for our needs should be reflected in the fellowship and behaviour of Christians. A few living in luxury while many are in poverty is destructive of community and contrary to the will of God. As Clement writes elsewhere, 'Goods are called goods because they do good, and they have been provided by God for the good of humanity' (Avila, 1983, 43).

In similiar vein, St Basil the Great (330–379) denies that there is any such thing as unconditional ownership; private property is simply an opportunity for 'beneficence and faithful distribution':

That bread which you keep, belongs to the hungry; that coat which you preserve in your wardrobe, to the naked; those shoes which are rotting in your possession, to the shoeless; that gold which you have hidden in the ground, to the needy. Wherefore, as often as you were able to help others, and refused, so often did you do them wrong (Avila, 1983, 50).

Ambrose of Milan (c. 334–397) sees almsgiving, what we would now call charity, as *restitution*:

Not from your own do you bestow upon the poor man, but you make return for what is his. For what has been given as common for the use of all, you appropriate to yourself

alone. The earth belongs to all, not to the rich . . . Therefore you are paying a debt, you are not bestowing what is not due (Avila, 1983, 66).
Redistribution of wealth is the restoration to the poor of what is properly, that is, according to the will of God, theirs.

John Chrysostom (c.347–407) is not afraid to declare that property unshared is theft: 'This is robbery; not to share one's resources' (Avila, 1983, 83). It is not that the Fathers are against property as such. But property is for use and for sharing, not for accumulation, avarice and luxury. And Chrysostom develops this point:

> Is not 'the earth is God's and the fulness thereof'? If then our possessions belong to one common Lord, they also belong to our fellow-servants. The possessions of one Lord are all common (Avila, 95).

For Augustine (354–430), possessions are to be used as means for our pilgrimage towards God. True possession involves right use, that is, use in accordance with God's will, use that encourages fellowship and sharing: 'What could be more unjust,' he asks, 'than to wax rich at the expense of another's growing poor?' (Avila, 117).

The middle ages were marked by a series of movements of protest against luxury in the midst of poverty which usually appealed to the Bible and Christian theology in presenting their case. Many were millenarian and heretical, but others remained within the mainstream of orthodoxy. Many of them are described and discussed in Norman Cohn's fascinating book, *The Pursuit of the Millenium*.

The sects which emerged among the poor in many parts of Europe were mostly egalitarian, looked upon private property as an evil and advocated evangelical poverty. The movement founded by Peter Waldus in Lyons in the late twelfth century spread rapidly over much of south Europe. Waldus' followers were often called the Poor Men of Lyons. Waldus himself was said to have been a rich merchant who distributed his possessions among the poor and advocated a return to primitive Christian styles of life. The Waldensians were viciously persecuted as heretics and finally survived only in the mountains of Piedmont, emerging at the time of the Reformation as a reformed church which had been established centuries before Luther and took the ethical precepts of the gospels more seriously than did the Lutheran reformation.

A wealthy church found such movements deeply threatening. A common charge against Waldensians or other Cathari was that they held goods in common and did not believe private property was acceptable for Christians.

Peasant protest movements against poverty and oppression were often led by 'poor priests' who preached a simple evangelical message which echoed the teaching of the Fathers centuries before. John Ball, a priest and leader of the Peasants' Revolt of 1381, was reputed to have preached a sermon to the rebels on the proverb: When Adam delved and Eve span, who was then the gentleman? Froissart claims that Ball said:

> Things cannot go well in England, nor ever will, until all goods are held in common, and until there will be neither serfs nor gentlemen, and we shall all be equal . . . If we are all descended from one father and one mother, Adam and Eve, how can they assert or prove that they are more masters than ourselves? (Morris, 1949, 34–5; Cohn, 1970, 201).

The Scottish Reformation was particularly closely related to popular protests against injustice, oppression and unfair distribution. Sir David Lindsay's play, *The Thrie Estaites*, revived so remarkably at the Edinburgh Festival, makes this abundantly clear as John Commonweal supported by Gude Counsel and Divine Correction denounces the exactions and exploitation of the nobility, the burgesses, and the church. Reformation in religion was clearly regarded as inseparable from reformation in society, and multitudes of people looked for a just society as well as a purified church. Popular support for the reformation was aroused both by the millenarian expectation of a just and fraternal society and by the determination to return as far as possible to the purity of an early church which took seriously evangelical teaching on sharing, care for the neighbour, and rejection of avarice. For a century or more after the Reformation, ministers were repeatedly enjoined to denounce from the pulpit the oppressions of the rich and powerful. It was assumed that the church stood with the poor, and stood for justice.

Whenever Christians have become aware of growing poverty and inequities in distribution there have been protests by individuals, by movements, and even by churches. Such is a necessary expression of what it means to be a prophetic faith.

(b) *Regulation* As soon as Christianity began to have political and social influence, attempts started to regulate the economy in the light of Christian faith. This was believed to be necessary in a fallen world, where men and women were usually only too willing to exploit their neighbours, or confuse their own interests with the common good. The weak and the poor required protection. Thus emerged one of the great intellectual achievements of the middle ages – the development of a sophisticated theory of the 'just price' and the 'just wage'.

Like the Bible and the early church, medieval theology viewed the economy with some suspicion, as a nursery of greed and covetousness with a strong inbuilt tendency towards injustice and luxury. For a few a 'better way' was possible, either in the embracing of holy poverty (as with the friars), or in a monastic community in which everything was held in common. But for most people life in the world involved compromising the absolute demands of the Christian ethic in order to take part in ordinary economic activity. Getting and spending, the creation of wealth, and market transactions required to be restrained, channelled and limited by churchly and theological oversight if they were to be acceptable. The economy shares in the fallenness of the world. An implication of this is that the procedures and structures through which wages and prices are set should be treated with respect, for they are necessary, but not with reverence, for they may be manipulated by the wealthy and powerful and do not of themselves generate justice. Regulation is required to exclude the ways in which people may profit at the expense of the poor.

Whatever we may think about such an overall assessment of the economic system, it certainly guards against any kind of idolization of the economy, any suggestion that economic institutions and processes are God-given and beyond human control or questioning, essentially beneficient if left to operate without interference, following their own laws. Nor is there in this way of thinking any place for the belief that 'self love and social be the same' (Pope), or that acquisitiveness is in some way a Christian virtue. Christian economic ethics constantly (and rightly) assumed that economic transactions were relations between people, and that people must accept responsibility before God for their economic behaviour.

The theological assumptions of just wage/just price theory were that God sustains an objective moral order; that it is he who accords worth and value to people and things; that he calls for right dealings in the economy as elsewhere in life; that he is the ultimate judge of those who act unjustly; and that God is committed to the special protection of the poor and the weak against the rich and powerful.

The ethical assumptions of the theory are that value has an objective existence apart from scarcity value, and should not be inflated or depressed by manipulation of the market or otherwise. Both utility and the labour required to produce an article were relevant criteria for assessing the 'objective value', and hence the just price; exchange value was not the only criterion, although it had to be taken into consideration. In settling prices and wages, account must be taken of the common good, not simply of the interests of the immediately involved parties. And, above all, wages and prices must express distributive justice.

A just wage must be at a level adequate to keep the labourer and the worker's family and spouse at the standard customary for their social class; wage earners must not be made into paupers, but enabled to live with dignity and decency, with the resources necessary for the fulfilment of their basic duties towards their families and society. Unlike the judgments of

God, human calculations of just prices or just wages must always be approximate. Individuals' calculations tend to be distorted by self-interest; it is better to make the fixing of levels of wages a matter of a kind of consensus within a society. As far as possible, there should be equal pay for equal work (Fogarty, 1961, 257–299).

This tradition of thought about the economy is realistic about ways in which power and wealth manipulate things to their advantage. It is one way of expressing an option for the poor, and asserting the dignity and rights of all human beings. In its day it was a proper and living expression of Christian responsibility. But it worked best in relatively simple societies with undeveloped economic institutions. And although it was suspicious of the *economy* it tended to accept the *social order* as a kind of given. Within a highly unequal and hierarchical social order the church expressed a concern for the poor and an opposition to ostentation and luxury; it attempted to mitigate the worst effects of the economic workings of a highly unequal society, but it did not question the social order or the overall pattern of distribution. In modern circumstances a care for just prices and just wages must be combined with policies designed to promote equity in the social order itself.

In the eighteenth and nineteenth centuries the churches almost abandoned efforts to regulate economic activity. Faced with the new world of capitalism, they failed to rethink the situation, and could only repeat old truths about moderation and the personal obligations of Christians within an unquestioned hierarchical social order.

Some in the churches began to deny that the economy was properly subject to moral control, and accepted the suggestion that any outside interference was harmful. But in our day, from the US Catholic Bishops, from the World Council of Churches, from the Vatican, from the Archbishop of Canterbury's Commission on Urban Priority Areas, from the liberation theologians of Latin America, from working parties such as ours and from many others has come a determined effort to articulate a Christian judgment on economic matters.

(c) *Alternative communities* Down the centuries the Christian church has produced a whole series of experiments in community living and in sharing, at once protests against the unjust state of the world, and demonstrations that other, fairer and more loving ways of living together are possible. This was an emphasis in the origins of monasticism. Even when wealth and decadence came to engulf some monasteries, the principle of community of goods persisted, a community which was supposed to reflect the life of Jesus with his disciples. The Franciscan friars went beyond community of goods – they embraced 'holy poverty' in order to share the lot of the poor and thus live close to the Lord. The Franciscan witness was deeply threatening to many in the church; things went so far that in 1323 the Pope issued a bull condemning the view that 'Our redeemer and Lord Jesus Christ and his apostles did not have anything, either privately or in common' (Mullin, 1983, 76). And lay communities as well often shared their belongings in order to experience a more evangelical style of life.

Every congregation of the church should regard itself as an experiment in community and in sharing. The church, after all, is called to be a sign of the Kingdom, a colony of heaven, a preliminary and partial manifestation of God's purposes, a demonstration of the truth and power of the gospel. All down the ages, the church has encouraged Christians to give with generosity to the poor, the weak, and those who suffer. Present day giving through Christian Aid, Tear Fund, or Oxfam is a continuation of a great tradition going back to the collection Paul sponsored for the poor of the Jerusalem church. And the church has a great tradition of care for the weak and the poor. In Scotland, for example, we remember Thomas Chalmers' attempts to restore a 'godly commonwealth' in urban Scotland through his work in the parish of St John's in Glasgow, and his establishment of new parishes in the slums of the great cities. Chalmers' work was, and is, controversial, but without entering into a discussion of his achievement we should note that he was convinced that questions of distribution were matters for the church. He believed that the community, not some outside agency, should care for its own poor and vulnerable members, and that the church should be at the heart of the community, sharing its concerns and problems. Poverty, he taught, should be prevented rather than relieved. In a way he was the first protagonist of the welfare society.

At the heart of the life of the church there is the sacrament of sharing, the Lord's Supper, when Christians take the cup and break the bread as a memorial of the one who said, according to St John's gospel, 'The bread which I give is my own flesh; I give it for the life of the world' (John 6.51). In the supper, the Lord shares himself with his people, and they share with one another. And those who share this bread and this cup are thereby committing themselves to sharing in joyful fellowship with the needy of the world, anticipating the messianic banquet and emulating the open-table fellowship of Jesus himself.

6.   Distribution in the Church of Scotland

Early on in our discussions we agreed in the working party that the church cannot stand in judgment on society without having had a thorough look at itself. Only too often the church has sided with the rich and powerful. In Scotland and England it is now largely a middle-class organization, concerned *for* the poor no doubt, but hardly anywhere a church *of* the poor. It is deeply compromised by its involvement with the economic and power structures of our society. The last few pages have given only one side of the history of the church, the side which has shown its faithfulness to the gospel. But the church again and again has co-operated with rather than confronted the 'principalities and powers'. The church has itself often been part of structures of oppression. It has failed to demonstrate an alternative way of sharing power and wealth and has simply mirrored and confirmed the unjust structures of society. These things need to be confronted.

How far does the church in the way it deploys its resources and pays its employees express the theological and ethical insights we have been discussing in this book? We will now examine the Church which commissioned this report, and to which most of the members of the working party belong, to see how far, if at all, the church makes a distinctive witness in matters of distribution.

Remuneration The Church of Scotland has no general policy on the remuneration of its staff. Historically, ministers' stipends were locally derived, largely through the system of teinds. This had the merit of linking stipend to the community's level of prosperity. But it also led to wide variations, with poor parishes with low stipends left in the hands of the incompetent or saintly! As recently as 1939, high stipends could be four times greater than those of the lower paid ministers, but since the introduction of the minimum stipend system, no minister is paid more than 50% above the minimum.

Individual stipends are decided by the Presbytery and the appropriate Assembly committee in consultation with the congregation. Any increase suggested by the congregation must be more than matched by increased payments to the Minimum Stipend Fund. Travelling and other expenses are the same for all ministers, although there is some scope for variation over secretarial help, etc. Each minister is provided with a manse, or an allowance instead, and thus pays no rent or rates.

It is hard to assess how the stipends of Church of Scotland ministers compare with the pay of other professions. Certainly ministers are not overpaid in comparison with social workers and teachers, and they have virtually no promotion possibilities. But there is high job security.

Does the present system direct human resources to the places of greatest need? Although there may be rewards other than financial from working in parishes in poor areas, such parishes are almost all on the minimum stipend with a small additional allowance. There may also be some pastoral assistance provided with funds from outside the parish. But in general the system means that if an experienced minister were to move to a housing scheme parish after some years in suburbia, it might mean a drop of £1–2,000 in stipend, just when family costs may be highest. A policy of bias to the poor would surely seek to reverse this.

It is in the payment of overseas staff that the most radical policy prevails. All staff, whatever their profession and qualifications, receive the same basic allowance. Adjustment is made between countries to ensure a similar standard of living, and there are special additions for dependents and for specific needs. Most overseas staff earn substantially less than they would for equivalent work at home – but in many countries a good deal more than their local colleagues.

In 1985 a new salary scheme was introduced for staff at the Church's headquarters, 121 George Street, Edinburgh. The new salaries took into account age (12.5%), service (12.5%), job content (50%), and merit rating (25%). To some extent the principles of the new system are similar to normal business practice, but salary levels are about 10% lower than for equivalent work outside.

In its stipends there has been a trend over the years towards a significant reduction in the differential between the top and the lowest stipends. This has been widely welcomed, and provides a striking contrast to the development of salary structures in most other institutions. Is it perhaps a sign of the Kingdom that a church can have a dedicated and hardworking cadre of ministers without the motivation of promotion and high salaries?

Wealth   The Church of Scotland, like other churches and institutions, has large assets. It has accumulated property and capital over the years. It has some land and many buildings, some of which seem more of a liability than a resource. How does the church use its wealth and its resources?

In the first place, it tends to take a long-term view of its responsibilities. It must think of generations yet to come. It holds these resources in trust for the future. And that is surely legitimate. But it is not enough, especially if it is simply the future of the institution that is in view. The church is steward of resources for the sake of the Kingdom. And the church has responsibilities to the community in which it is set.

Accordingly some congregations have begun to see the potential of their buildings, which are often very underused, for community service. With the help of MSC funds, a variety of projects to make the church's buildings more of an asset to the whole community have been undertaken. But there is scope for a complete reappraisal of the use of church property for mission and service to the needs of our society.

In other countries in recent years there have been instances of churches giving away land or buildings to help the poor. In the Caribbean, church land has been given to young people to farm as co-operatives. In the United States, church bodies have begun to make available property for the use of disadvantaged groups. In the aftermath of the report on *Faith in the City* the Church of England has established a fund to help in the establishment of community projects in areas of multiple deprivation. These may be little more than gestures which only affect a tiny percentage of the church's total resources, and do not confront the structures of maldistribution. But gestures may be signs, tokens of the church's commitment to the Kingdom.

The Church of Scotland Trust administers the central assets of the church, and many congregations place their reserves and investments with the Trust. This was established in 1932, and the trustees control three funds:

(*a*) The General Investment Fund, amounting to about £67 million, is designed for longterm investment, combining capital growth and income.

(*b*) The Income Fund, valued at about £23 million, offers a more attractive yield, with less capital growth.

(*c*) The Deposit Fund, worth about £20 million, is intended for short-term investment, and pays a quarterly dividend.

The trustees in managing these funds give priority to strictly financial considerations, but on principle they do not invest in companies involved in brewing, distilling, tobacco manufacture, or gambling. Under pressure from the General Assembly, they do not now invest directly in South Africa or in companies with a substantial stake in the South African economy. While they have been reluctant to bring pressure themselves on companies in which they have investments concerning moral issues, they have not objected to the church approaching companies to urge disinvestment from South Africa. In short, the church manages its capital resources in a conventional manner, seeking the best return, but willing to mitigate that policy in particular instances in response to particularly strong arguments from within the church.

A different approach to investment is offered by the Ecumenical Development Co-operative Society, founded by the World Council of Churches, which aims to direct church funds to investment in projects among the world's poor. Since operations started in 1975, a fund worth over £8 million has been built up, offering loans at modest rates of interest to model projects among the poor, and offering investors a very much more modest return than they would get on the market. In Scotland a company has been set up, with representatives of the different churches as trustees, to encourage individuals and churches to put money into the EDCS.

Such initiatives are, of course, tiny. And the sums that have been reinvested for moral reasons are negligible. It would be hard to argue that the Church of Scotland, or other churches for that matter, has an investment strategy which in any way reflects distinctively Christian criteria. It does not show a bias to the poor, nor does it challenge the structures of unjust distribution that offend the Christian conscience.

The church is people, and congregations, not just an institution. We cannot say what guidance, if any, is given from the pulpit about Christian ways of getting, and spending, and sharing. We do not know how many groups discuss how Christians should deal with their investments, and their pay, and how congregations should deploy their resources for the sake of God's Kingdom. We have not explored how often levels of benefit, or taxation, or overseas aid, or policies towards poverty and deprivation, are discussed in presbyteries, assemblies and kirk sessions. We hope this

book will help some Christians to give informed attention to
these matters. For they impinge upon the Kingdom of God
and the mission of the church.

The Christian tradition which we have explored in this
chapter challenges some common attitudes to questions of
distribution and suggests some reasons why the way things
are shared is spiritually important. We do not find in this
tradition a blueprint of the good society, but it does call for
fundamental questioning of much that is happening in our
society and in the world today. And it suggests a vision of
sharing fellowship which is capable of providing a general
orientation for policy.

With this in mind we return to the contemporary situation
to ask what, in the light of the Christian vision, can be done
to encourage more fair, loving and neighbourly sharing.

Chapter Four

SHARING IN ACTION

1 Introduction

Our exploration of the Christian tradition has provided some guidance as to our response to the situations described in Chapters One and Two. This response, we think, must be in terms of action in three related areas – personal lifestyle, the way the church organizes its own sharing and distribution, and public policy.

Many people feel impotent in face of the problems of the world. But there are things that we can do. We can change our way of life so that it indicates that we are committed to sharing and to fellowship. If we are Christians, we can try to ensure that the church is a kind of experiment in just sharing. We can develop a sensitivity to the patterns of distribution that are supported by our trade unions, professional organizations and institutions, with a special eye to how the weakest and the poorest are treated. And in public policy there are many things which could be done immediately to help the poor and improve things in areas of deprivation. What is needed is the will and the vision.

Unless we each examine our own use of possessions, how we feel about sharing things, and how we relate to structures of distribution in which we are involved, we have no right to expect institutions to follow standards more stringent than those we apply to ourselves. The church as a sign and foretaste of the Kingdom should demonstrate in the way its own life is arranged that it takes seriously the values of the Kingdom, and show that just and gracious distribution strengthens fellowship and love. Only on this basis is it credible for Christians to suggest ways in which the nation might better arrange its distribution.

Some see no unfairness but only fair reward for effort in our present structures of distribution. Some experience its unfairness directly: they live in poverty. The experience of others is indirect: they are personally adequately provided for, but they are uneasy about unfairness to those around them.

Concerned people are often uncertain what to do. We are afraid; fearful for our own security and that of our family; afraid that change might go too far, and we might find ourselves worse off, or committed to a more radical sharing than we find easily acceptable. But poor people are afraid too, afraid of the continuance of poverty, afraid of what it means for them and their families.

The facts of distribution make us variously angry, frightened or threatened. For our own interests and possessions are involved. This makes it particularly difficult to bring every thought and prejudice and attitude into captivity to Christ – yet it is precisely this that Christians are called upon to do. And only so may they make a distinctive contribution.

The best way of replacing fear with confidence is by building trust in the fairness and justice of our social arrangements and systems of distribution. Christians should surely be bold enough to point to the injustice of our present patterns of distribution, and suggest better ways of arranging things. This may not be easy. But keeping quiet may mean a poorer life for our neighbours.

Since Christians believe in the corrupting effects of sin on structures as well as people, they do not think that entrenched structures of power and wealth will capitulate without a struggle to an ethic of love and fellowship. We agree with the Anglican report, *Not Just for the Poor* (1987), that 'Extremes of wealth and poverty are a consequence of sin, and witness to the conscious or unconscious capacity for injustice of the rich and powerful, and the consequent disintegration of society. The way society responds to the poor is a crucial test of its moral health' (27). An ethic of justice is needed, and in a fallen world sometimes it is necessary to compromise in the pursuit of principle. Christians are not utopians, for they take power, and the corruptions of power, very seriously. They are as interested in little steps towards a better world as they are in grand ideals. Principles need to be struggled for. Power must be harnessed if principles are to be implemented. And entrenched interests resist a more just ordering of society. But Christian faith gives resources and motivation to struggle against the 'principalities and powers', and enjoins a 'bias to the poor'.

2   Perspectives

(a) *Love*   Towering above all other principles is that of love (Agape), supremely expressed in the Incarnation. The Love Commandment (Luke 10.27) sets the tone of any Christian approach to life. Love demands equal concern for all people in their uniqueness and their relationships. Unlike the formal principle of Justice – that all should be treated equally unless there is some overriding reason not to – love positively seeks the good in and of others, seeking to affirm them and enable them to develop. Love demands no precondition of desert or of merit. For Christians, distribution is inextricably linked with relationships and their flourishing. Sharing expresses Love.

Love means that there must be a concern for how distribution takes place and for the quality of attitudes and relationships among givers and receivers. Does a particular mechanism of distribution demean the recipients or corrupt the givers, or does it affirm them and their human dignity? Does it encourage and enable them to be full participant members of the community?

(b) *Community*   Distribution occurs within community. Membership of a community expresses the loving acceptance of the interdependence of human beings. In community, people share responsibility for one another, loving their neighbours as themselves. For if the acceptance of inter-dependence is truly informed by Love, then the sharing of responsibility naturally follows.

The perspective of community demands the institutionali-
zation of the sharing of resources in response to shared
needs. All members of the community have a right to share
in the community's resources. At this point, the principle of
commonwealth supplants that of community, embodying the
idea that all material resources were created for all. They
were created for all for the purpose of fostering true fellowship in the community and for the well-being of each and
every individual. We argue that the sharing of material
resources is an expression of fellowship, and that excessive
inequality of distribution divides communities, and limits
freedom.

Identity should be discovered, and responsibility taken,
within a framework of mutually caring relationships. Values
learned in such a community will allow a true welfare society
to develop, as distinct from a system of state welfare in
which a needing majority are kept in a state of unhealthy
dependence. People need to feel that they are valued by
other members of their society if they are to develop self-
reliance and self-respect. We know – or we should do – when
raising our *own* children that a secure, loving, protected early
environment breeds confidence and the capacity to take
risks. People are not frightened into courage. Surely the
same applies to society as a whole.

(c) *Freedom*   Freedom likewise reflects an aspect of Love –
the concern for others in their uniqueness, a concern that
they be allowed to develop to their full. Freedom accords
people control over their own lives, and opportunities to
reach out. A positive freedom is not licence to do as one will,
and neither is it the negative protection of the individual's
independence from interference. This emphasises only one
dimension of the principle of freedom – respect for autonomy
– while ignoring the fact that a proper distribution of resources
is necessary to encourage autonomy and enable its development. Freedom is properly developed and exercised in
fellowship, not in isolation.

Freedom is often seen in terms of extending the range of

choices facing the individual. It is possible for poor people to 'get by' with a measure of independence and dignity, but the stark truth is that within poverty, access to social and material goods and the power to control one's life in a responsible way are severely restricted. As the *Faith in the City* Report has it:

[The poor] are trapped in housing and in environments over which they have little control. They lack the means and opportunity – which so many of us take for granted – of making choices in their lives (Archbishop's Commission, 1985, xv).

People must have the power and the space to control and develop their lives within the fabric of a community which has its own claims upon the individual. Freedom should not be seen as freedom to escape from society and responsibilities to the neighbour.

These perspectives suggest ground rules for a balanced and fair society in which individuals can be respected for what they are, can take responsibility with and through the state for caring and are trusted to make their own decisions, individually and as a community.

Our priorities in distribution must begin with the poor and the powerless. The term 'bias to the poor' (cf. Sheppard, 1983) may be held to be unfortunate in implying an advocacy of treatment that is not scrupulously even-handed. But making a priority out of concern for the poor is an expression of justice, a way of redressing deep-seated unfairnesses, and so a sign of hope for everyone in society.

Those with the least power who should be the subject of priority concern include:

(*i*) Those who require some kind of sheltered environment, such as children, the elderly, the infirm or the disabled and in general those who cannot cope adequately without help and care.

(*ii*) Those who take on the primary responsibility for caring. Women are particularly vulnerable because of the expectation in society that they will perform most of the unpaid caring tasks.

(*iii*) Those who cannot participate in the labour market on a full-time basis, including both the above groups as well as those who are unemployed or retired.

(*iv*) Those whose wage-rate is so low that it is insufficient to meet their basic living costs. This adds many who are victims of discrimination on the basis of race or gender, and many who are simply unskilled or inexperienced.

Objectives From this perspective clear objectives emerge which can form the basis of actions. These include:

(*a*) The encouragement of community, especially through the provision of opportunities for service and participation. This de-emphasises materialism and the individualist ethic, and looks to rewards other than financial.

(*b*) The provision of a minimum income sufficent to allow the individual to have access to the 'goods' the community regards as necessary.

(*c*) The narrowing of the range of distribution of income and wealth.

(*d*) The humanization of state distribution so as to do away with the stigma and discrimination of means testing.

(*e*) An effective education for autonomy – not just in schools, but in the community and at the crucial points of distribution, such as in the NHS. There must be preparation for a greater emphasis on democracy, such that individuals and communities can assume responsibility for themselves.

Equitable distribution that allows individuals to develop must go hand in hand with the building of community, the sharing of responsibility, and grass-roots democracy.

3 Lifestyle

Changes in lifestyle can have an important symbolic or demonstrative effect, showing that there are many things that we take for granted which do not have to be accepted. People who live differently may become trendsetters, arousing the curiosity of others and encouraging them to examine their own lives in a fresh light. Changes in lifestyle can thus help to alter or remove attitudes which sustain the way in which resources are distributed at present.

For Christians, changes of lifestyle concerned with the distribution of income and wealth can be considered in terms of four important dimensions of life – prayer, prophecy, political action and personal moderation (Dammers, 1986, 45).

(a) *Prayer*   Christian commitment to fair distribution begins with prayer. Prayer in this context must not be understood as a convenient escape route, leading from the distressing realities of this world into an other-worldly reality of heavenly peace and eternal harmony.

Prayer is not for escapists, but for bridge-builders. In prayer we do not follow the dreamer's route out of the world: we follow Christ's route into the world, thus bridging the deep gap between the reality of God's love on the one hand, and the unholy reality of maldistribution, injustice and human suffering on the other.

This path is not an easy one to walk. It was not easy for Christ, and it is not easy for those who are prepared to follow him in prayer and in action. It is a path which leads to the cross – and beyond. The cross is the ultimate symbol of the clash between the Kingdom of God, the caring community of love which Jesus came to inaugurate, and the powers of the world, which see this kingdom and its representative as threatening to their own interests. The cross encapsulates the world's rejection of God's offer of a community of sharing. If we pray for the coming of the Kingdom, we inevitably enter that conflict. We taste the pain of the cross. Prayer means allowing the pain of rejection, of injustice and maldistribution, to enter into the centre of our beings.

But prayer is more than that. Christ's story did not end with rejection and pain and brokenness: it was turned by God into hope. The cross also becomes the ultimate symbol of expectation because God raised the crucified Christ after three days, and in doing so vindicated him. There is hope, a future of justice, sharing and fellowship, for God has turned the cross from a symbol of pain and conflict into a symbol of liberation and hope.

Prayer for sharing, rooted in the cross of Christ, is thus both painful and liberating. It cannot be one without being the other.

To pray in this way means to offer to God the often appalling reality of maldistribution with true compassion and understanding. Important for such understanding is the attempt to identify those who are victims of poverty and who bear the brunt of our divided society, and to try to understand their position inside out. What does it feel like to be in their condition?

To identify with the victims in their plight is to become aware of the costs of our present patterns of distribution. Only if we are prepared to put ourselves in the victims' shoes, to learn what it is like to be without basics, to learn the price that they pay in terms of anxiety, ill-health and hopelessness – only then does our prayer become an expression of love. By getting in touch with the often hidden and silent suffering of our neighbours, we engage in the same work of love as Jesus when he encountered the suffering crowds, and felt for them 'in his guts' (Matt. 9.36).

Prayer at a safe distance is nonsense. Prayer changes the one who prays. We cannot pray without self-examination, feeling how we are implicated in the suffering of others, prolonging their agony through the roles that we play in society. We cannot pray for sharing without also addressing our own ingrown resistance to better distribution, facing our fears of losing privilege and power, questioning our own 'needs', our own dreams of what we would like to 'have', our own tendency to make allowances for ourselves that we would not make for other people. Prayer is painful because it involves the difficult process of personal reassessment.

But prayer for sharing is liberating and enabling as well as painful. In prayer, God meets us with his reconciling spirit, enabling us to move on from experiences of shock, anger or guilt to a dedicated commitment to change. We can clarify starting points and find new ways of re-shaping our world so that it comes to resemble more the promised future of a sharing community of neighbours. Prayer enables us to build bridges into God's future.

Prayer enables us to find the source and meaning of our existence in God rather than in our possessions. It alerts us to our deep-seated materialism, and makes us aware of its inadequacy. It thus sets us free to work for more equality and effective sharing with persistence. We are given tenacity, a strong sense of purpose, an ability to make sacrifices and to ask others to make sacrifices. Prayer for sharing triggers off a determined, intelligent and creative process of witnessing for a new community, linking us in partnership with all who share that vision. To 'Pray the Kingdom' is not something which happens easily. As Charles Elliott has pointed out, it requires work, a fresh approach which is both creative and disciplined (Elliott, 1985).

(b) *Prophecy* Prayer leads to prophecy. Prayer brings us to experience the painful tension between the power of God's spirit of community and the conditions of the world which contradict and deny any such community; prophecy is the way to bring that tension into the open, pointing out those structures and circumstances which cause Christ to be cruci-fied again and again in our world. The encounter in prayer with the cross compels the Christian to prophesy. It would be impossible to pray for greater fairness and more sharing and at the same time stand on the sidelines. Prophecy artic-ulates both the pain and the hope which can be experienced in prayer. Prophecy is witness to the community of the faith-ful and to the world at large, where God's offer of justice and peace is continually being rejected, of the vision of the com-ing of the future commonwealth which has started in Christ and which will come in its fullness. It *denounces* practices of maldistribution, and *announces* that Christ has come so that there may be justice for all in God's kingdom.

Prophecy is not only a matter of speaking out, although that is certainly a crucial part of it. There is also prophetic action. The prophets of the Old Testament frequently accompanied their words with striking and unusual actions which gave urgency and credibility to their message. If prophecy is to be more than talk, it must be mirrored in the lifestyle of the prophet. Christians should not only talk about community, but should live it, becoming living examples of the fact that it is possible to live that way. Christians should not only complain about the injustice of many having too little while a few have too much, but should be prepared themselves to make experiments of sharing. They should not only preach that having more and more does not make you of necessity more and more happy, but they should be prepared themselves to become signs of simplicity. A prophetic lifestyle makes the message concrete, more compelling and more credible.

The prophet must know what he is talking about. Uninformed generalities can easily become irrelevant bland declarations without cutting edge. The power and gift of the biblical prophets lay in the fact that they sensed where the roots of the problems faced by their contemporaries were, and were thus able to speak to the point in a way that made sense to their listeners. Prophecy has to be informed, and that means for the modern prophet speaking on matters of sharing that he must know the facts about maldistribution.

In particular, this involves speaking with and for those whose voices are not normally heard, but who are the real 'experts' on the reality of distribution in our society. Listening to the unheard and helping them to be heard is an important prophetic task today. As our opening chapter shows, description from within the reality of poverty and deprivation can be more telling than any number of statistics. Christian prophecy must help people to become aware of what unfair distribution can mean for other people's lives.

It is not a prophetic virtue to tiptoe around contentious issues when things need to be called by their true name. The causes and agents of maldistribution must be identified.

There must be protest when the ideologists of the day claim 'Peace, peace' when there is no peace, and when economic 'prosperity' is reached at an unacceptably high social cost. Prophets must speak out when freedom for some means deprivation and suffering for others.

(c) *Political action*   Prayer is but pious platitude if it is not an alignment for action, and prophecy is empty rhetoric if its words are left to die on the wind. The Christian is enjoined to obey the will of God, that it may be done, and obedience is centrally a matter of listening. A major characteristic of Jesus' ministry is his obedience, his listening in prayer to know the will of the Father, and then to do it. In prayer, we too should listen, to know God's will. The doing of that will, in the community, is the political action of which we are speaking here.

Jesus in his ministry proclaimed the Kingdom of God. This Kingdom was not an abstraction, or simply a spiritual renewal in the individual heart. It was, and is, a condition of social relationships realized in and through him, in a time of violence, oppression and alienation. Faithfulness to the Kingdom involves the transformation of the world by God's love and justice. And that is a political act. Father Cullinan calls this 'the obedience of political love' (Cullinan, 1982).

Jesus acted to bring in and include the outcasts and the alienated. Obedient Christian action will question radically those many aspects of existing social structures that tend to alienate and exclude. The justice that requires this inclusiveness does not always seem fair – at least not to those satisfied with the current state of affairs. The Prodigal Son's brother was quite understandably put out that his father had never thrown a party for him after years of faithful service!

It is probably easiest for individuals to channel their political energies if they confine themselves to defined objectives. In other words, people are drawn to single issue campaigns. We cannot prescribe what such campaigns should be for the individual Christian, but we can suggest criteria:

(*i*) Does a campaign promote inclusiveness, drawing the excluded back into fellowship?

(*ii*) Does it have a 'bias to the poor', affecting the distribution of power and wealth in the community in favour of the dispossessed?

These two criteria are interrelated. Inclusiveness is unlikely to be promoted if distribution is not at the same time tilted towards the poor. Such a tilt is of little value to the community if it is accomplished as an act of patronage that does not give the dispossessed greater control over their own lives. Our actions affecting others in accordance with God's will should rather be actions of what Cullinan calls 'political love'.

Campaigning on an issue such as homelessness clearly passes muster when judged by such criteria. Other issues, such as those concerned with the environment, may require an intervening layer of argument before they can be related to criteria of inclusiveness or of distribution. Sometimes issues will arise over which Christians, speaking their truth, will collide.

Single issue campaigns have their limitations. They rarely reach to the roots of the problem, and only occasionally affect the very structures of society. Even legislative outcomes from single-issue campaigns are unlikely to do more than mitigate circumstances. Perhaps Christian political love should rather address itself to 'general causes'.

The principal vehicle for influencing the 'general causes' of British politics is the political parties. Some interest groups may be so broad in their scope and so fundamental in the issues that they address that they should also be treated in this category. The 'peace movement' and the 'green movement' are like that. So, perhaps, is trade unionism. The churches, too, should not be discounted as political agents in their own right affecting society's 'general causes' – although we would not want anyone to use this observation as an excuse for not getting their hands dirty elsewhere!

The Christian must be prepared to work within the structures of the real world, and yet not be bound by them. A true 'vertical' orientation should allow a commitment to action that does not become trapped within secular structures.

Individuals, as we have often said, are fulfilled within communities, and communities are composed of people. The focus of Christian political action must necessarily be upon people and their relationships, and we must not lose sight of this as we grapple with institutions. We have been critical of the individualist theological and political Right, and we are equally disturbed by those on the Left who too readily subsume the interests of people within collective institutions and then make the interests of those institutions paramount.

Christians, then, are called to political action by their understanding, in obedience, of communion and community. The love to which their obedience leads them will compel them to act. This action in pursuit of the Kingdom will involve them in the imperfect structures of the real world. It will also frequently lead them into ridicule as 'fools for God' and into the pain of rejection. In many cases it may lead to the humiliation of 'trouble'. The Christian political activist has no easy, structured ideology upon which to fall back. There is nothing in the Gospel which tells us whether it would be right to raise Income Tax in order to pay for more council houses, or whether membership of NATO is conducive to the good of the community. The Christian must obey what prayer and the example of Jesus tell him to be right for the community.

(d) *Personal moderation* The example of personal lifestyle may be the surest way in which anyone and everyone may proclaim their commitment to the values of the Kingdom. Excesses of wealth and poverty result in exclusion from the community, and a lifestyle which recognizes this and which respects the value of community will be a lifestyle of moderation.

There is nothing wrong with money itself. But it is hard for a rich man to enter the Kingdom of God (Luke 18.25), basically because of the temptation for those who possess money to use it in selfish ways. We must not disregard ourselves, but judge what is appropriate for ourselves by first prayerfully appreciating the needs of our neighbours around us. We must live in such a way as not to deny others.

Moderation should not itself be conspicuous, and how the individual pursues it will vary in emphasis. Some will focus on expenditure and personal sharing. Others will express their commitment to sharing by striving to live with ecological efficiency, consuming the minimum of non-renewable resources. All should be guided to live hospitably, and in harmony with their surroundings.

Moderation in personal lifestyle means 'living simply that others may simply live'. It should be a way of recognizing that the hungry, the poor and the powerless are our neighbours, and that our patterns of consumption affect them. In addition to generous giving, this involves a call for simple moderation, for a life without waste or 'conspicuous consumption'. But the actual pattern of personal consumption may be less important than the relationships that underlie it. The Christian must be sensitive to the role of money in bringing a distorting power dimension into human relationships. Giving is a one-sided action. The requirement is to share, with love.

This has implications for family life. Is the allocation of resources within the household openly discussed and agreed by consensus? How is income inequality handled? Is there sharing? And if both partners work, how is the unpaid domestic work allocated? What value is put by the earners on the unpaid work performed by others, and is the unpaid work shared?

Many everyday practices at work infringe principles of loving neighbourliness. People should ask themselves a number of practical questions ... Am I on the fiddle in any way? Is my overtime robbing someone else of work? Am I being honest about my tax liability? Do I respond in my lifestyle to the injustices of the world?

Life is to be celebrated. The search for a moderate lifestyle should not make us gloomy. Sharing in the community is no sharing at all if it is not convivial. It is important to emphasize the positive ways in which we can make our lives a celebration of relationships with others.

4   Sharing in the life of the Church

Proposals coming from the church for a more equitable way of distributing the nation's wealth and resources will only carry credibility if the church itself adopts and practises equitable policies for the conduct of its own life. It is significant that the report of the Archbishop of Canterbury's Commission, *Faith in the City*, which received much publicity for its forthright criticisms of government policy, began with thirty-eight proposals for reform within the church before tabling twenty-three proposals concerning the life of the nation.

If it be true that 'if one member of the body suffers, the whole body suffers with it', then the Church of Scotland – and other churches – must find ways of interpreting and applying this to its whole organization as well as within congregations. Thus, we welcome the trend towards narrowing of the gap between the highest and the lowest stipends, with richer congregations supporting poorer when it comes to the provision of stipends.

This narrowing of the gap in stipends is commendable, but may not be enough. A case can be made for positive discrimination in the deployment of resources, so that more is allocated to points of greatest need and weakness. If those ministering in the name of the church in deprived areas were to receive more support than their fellows in richer areas, then a significant witness would be made about how God calls us to use and to share his resources.

The Church of Scotland already has a significant input into areas of multiple deprivation through Community Ministers, Social Responsibility Schemes and now through MSC projects. This commitment would, we believe, be enhanced and increased by the setting up of a special fund to encourage and 'pump-prime' further community projects in such areas – a step which has been proposed by the Anglican report on *Faith in the City*.

Involvement of richer congregations in this way in the preferential support of areas of deprivation is not, we believe, merely a matter of material justice, but could prove to be a powerful stimulus to spiritual life.

A major capital resource of any organization is its buildings. The church is well endowed in this respect. *Faith in the City* challenges Christians to reappraise the use of buildings and land, putting them more positively at the disposal of the community and of organizations of all kinds. There is need for such reappraisal in Scotland, and we welcome the lead given in this respect by a number of congregations. Church buildings, especially in areas of deprivation, represent a significant resource that the church can share with the community of which it is a part.

Is there not an opportunity for the Christian church to demonstrate new principles of lending, emphasising criteria of need? Various alternative forms of investment are available to investors, lending money to meet the needs of people, although bearing interest at less than commercial rates. These funds allow much-needed projects to get off the ground – and in future these may bear fruit in both material and spiritual returns. Congregations might look to such fraternal placing of at least a portion of their capital funds.

5 Public policy

We believe that there is need for a 'Great Debate' about distribution. People need to be better informed about present patterns of distribution, about the choices before the nation, and about the implications of decisions which might be taken for the future of our society. We need to overcome ignorance and prejudice, and probe beneath the polarized positions of the political parties. Something like a 'New Beveridge Report' could provide the basis for such a debate. The agenda for such an enquiry would need to include the following issues:

(a) *Integrating the social security and taxation systems* At present, our social security and taxation systems are independent of each other and unco-ordinated. The most persistent anomaly arising from this is the 'poverty trap', whereby some recipients of benefit find themselves paying an effective tax rate greater than 100%. The integration of the two systems would prevent the taxation of incomes close to the poverty line and remove the poverty trap.

(b) *Reducing dependence upon means-tested benefits* There should be a move away from means-tested benefits (MTBs) towards benefits as of right – which should in turn be distinguished from National Insurance benefits dependent on contribution records and entitlement conditions. A move away from MTBs would help to reduce the stigma of receiving benefit, and would improve rates of take-up of benefits by those needing them.

Because of the way in which MTBs taper off as income rises, they constitute a major regressive element in the tax and benefits structure, whereby poorer people face a higher marginal tax rate than those with higher incomes. High marginal tax rates on low income trap people in poverty, reduce incentives to earn, and have a divisive effect on society.

(c) *Introduction of a lower rate tax band* A lower rate tax band on lower slices of income would help to make the personal tax system more progressive, and would reduce marginal tax rates among the low paid. If a priority is to help those living in poverty or on its margins, then the current preoccupation with reducing the standard rate of income tax is misplaced; a lower rate band at the threshold of tax payment would do more to help people trying to escape from poverty.

(d) *Reducing tax reliefs and allowances* The complex system of tax reliefs operating in Britain tends to make the tax system more regressive in general, as the reliefs benefit those earning enough to be liable to pay significant amounts of personal tax. Similarly, the raising of tax thresholds is regressive in that it only benefits those with an income greater than the old threshold. Tax reliefs diminish the tax base on which taxes are levied, resulting in higher tax rates having to be set to raise the same amount of revenue. The married man's allowance and the system of tax relief on mortgage interest payments both serve massively to reduce the tax base, and their phasing out should be considered, with a first step being the limitation of all tax reliefs to the standard rate of tax.

(*e*) *Consideration of schemes for tax credit, social dividend and basic income*   There are a number of possible ways of recasting the whole system of distribution which deserve serious and careful consideration. Some of them were outlined and discussed in Tony Walter's book *Fair Shares?* (1985). The issues are very complex, but it is important that we should not feel totally boxed into the present system, and should investigate alternatives.

(*f*) *Introduction of a wealth tax*   The main method by which wealth is concentrated in families over generations is by gifts and inheritances. Taxation of such transfers of wealth between individuals is so easy to avoid legally in Britain, given the allowances and exemptions for Capital Transfer Tax, as to be derisory. A more effective system needs to be devised if we are to avoid the perpetuation of current concentrations of wealth. Meanwhile, a move towards taxing transfers as part of the income of the recipient rather than as part of the giver's estate would help to disperse transfers more widely. In addition, it is time to reconsider the implementation of a wealth tax, taxing not just the income from capital concentrations, but attempting to redistribute the concentrations themselves.

(*g*) *Reform of housing finance*   Financial assistance with housing is in a state of confusion. The privileges and penalties applying to the different sectors of the housing market – owner-occupied, private rented and public rented – constitute a system displaying considerable inequities. The subsidies available to owner-occupied housing are such as to put owners in receipt of considerably more subsidy over a lifetime than is received by a council tenant, and the owner-occupier ends up with a substantial capital asset. We need fairness in the grant of financial assistance as between owner-occupied and rented sectors, with subsidy allocated relative to the needs of the householders in each sector. In general, the claim of the rented sectors on the public purse must be greater because of the needs of so many of the tenants and because of the inferior state of so much of the housing stock in question.

(*h*) *Commitment to an increase in development aid*   Concerned though we rightly are with inequalities within our own wealthy society, we must not forget the greater inequalities that exist on a global scale. Our own government should act to ensure that our development aid budget is deployed in the interests of the world's poorest people, and is not diverted in pursuit of our own political or trading interests. British development aid should rise quickly to 1% of GNP, and we must play a positive role in promoting reforms of inter-national trading agreements so that developing countries are less disadvantaged in their trading relationships. The long-term goal for the world economy which Britain should help to promote is the New International Economic Order of which the Brandt Report speaks.

Meanwhile we believe that there are some policies which could be immediately adopted and which would help to prevent poverty in old age, in families, among the long-term unemployed, and among the disabled. We did not, of course, have the time or the expertise to consider the whole field of policies of distribution. But these proposals seem to us to be ways of expressing Christian values in today's Britain.

6   Urgent priorities

(*a*) *Extending the higher long-term rate of Supplementary Benefit to the unemployed*   Revitalizing the economy and restructur-ing industry are necessary for the good of the nation as a whole. But the families of the unemployed bear a particularly heavy share of the cost of economic and social change. They are the victims of change, and deserve some compensation. We can see no justification for denying the long-term unemployed the higher long-term rate of Supplementary Benefit.

(b) *Increasing the level of Child Benefit* Children are the future of the nation. But far too many grow up deprived and in poverty, without a fair chance in life and with a sense of exclusion. Families with children have a high risk of poverty, and the statistics show that child poverty is indeed increasing. There is wide support for Child Benefit, and we believe it should be substantially increased.

(c) *Increase in basic pension* The priority in pensions should be to help the poorest pensioners who have no occupational pension to top up their state pension. About a third of pensioners live in poverty, and they are predominantly females over 75. Many have difficulty in heating their homes in winter. Anything which would make them less dependent upon means-tested Supplementary Benefit with its problems of invasion of privacy, stigma and low take-up (so that many who need help do not get it) is to be welcomed. We believe that there should be a substantial increase in the basic pension.

(d) *Introduction of a National Disability Income* The disabled have more than enough problems in managing their lives without having also to cope with poverty. There is a strong case for changing the basis of benefit from the cause of disability – war, industrial injury, accident, medical side-effect, and so on – to the degree and cost of the disability. There should be a basic income for the disabled, plus a payment to cover the costs of disability. There should also be more generous care allowances for the disabled.

(e) *Family impact statements* As part of moves towards increasing its accountability to the electorate, the government should be required to add 'family impact statements' to all policy proposals. Such a practice would not in itself make the government accountable, since stated intention and actual effect often diverge widely, but people would then be able to judge government actions more perceptively.

These measures would, we recognize, be expensive. Although they are all urgent and desirable, they might need to be phased in over a period. Even if the country achieves a high rate of economic growth, they would need to be financed through higher taxation of the middle and upper income groups. We have suggested already that Christians should be willing to pay higher taxes. And if unemployment is reduced there will be a large increase in revenue. A high level of unemployment is immensely costly to the nation in financial as well as human terms.

Most of our recommendations have concerned taxation and benefits. But these are ways of putting right, or reducing the harm, of an extremely unequal system of distribution whereby some top industrialists and financiers have salaries of over £1,000,000 a year, while student nurses draw only £4,540, and many people who are earning are still in poverty. Such extreme inequalities are impossible to justify. If most people were employed at decent wages, the social budget would be much reduced.

In this chapter we have been concerned with the question of how to respond to what we have found – in other words, how do we respond to Jesus Christ and the neighbours he has given us in today's world? We have argued that the only credible response must be on three related fronts:

our personal life-style – how do we deal with our possessions and open ourselves to the need around us?

the life of the church – how may each congregation be an experiment in community and sharing, and the whole church provide a foretaste of the just sharing and fellowship of the Kingdom?

and *in national policy* – how may the nation best express its respect for the dignity and value of each person and establish structures of just sharing? This last is particularly contentious ground, but Christians and citizens of a democracy cannot responsibly refuse to enter it. There are things we can do, and choices which must be taken. We need to help people to rise above a sense of fatalism and impotence.

This book is intended to encourage a process of study, prayer and action on matters of distribution. Just sharing is the will of God and the work of the Kingdom. Poor people and those working in areas of deprivation often wonder 'Who cares?' Christians must show in action and in prayer that they care.

REFERENCES

M.S. Ahluwalia, 'Income Inequality: Some Dimensions of the Problem' in H. Chenery et al., *Redistribution with Growth*, Oxford University Press 1974

Archbishop's Commission on Urban Priority Areas, *Faith in the City*, Church House Publishing 1985

Charles Avila, *Ownership: Early Christian Teaching*, Sheed and Ward 1983

Karl Barth, *Church Dogmatics*, Vol. 1/2, T & T Clark 1956

Brandt Commission, *North–South: A Programme for Survival*, Pan 1980

Church of England Board for Social Responsibility, *Not Just for the Poor*, Church House Publishing 1987

Norman Cohn, *The Pursuit of the Millenium*, Paladin 1970

Thomas Cullinan, *The Passion of Political Love*, Catholic Institute for International Relations 1982

Horace Dammers, *A Christian Life Style*, Hodder and Stoughton 1986

A. Deacon and J. Bradshaw, *Reserved for the Poor*, Blackwell 1983

David Donnison, *The Politics of Poverty*, Martin Robertson 1982

J.C. Duarte, 'Aspectos da Distribuicao no Brasil em 1970', cited in R. Heatley, *Poverty and Power*, Zed 1979

Charles Elliott, *Praying the Kingdom: Towards a Political Spirituality*, Darton, Longman and Todd 1985

Charles Elliott, *Comfortable Compassion? Poverty, Power and the Church*, Hodder and Stoughton 1987

Leon Epsztein, *Social Justice in the Ancient Near East and the People of the Bible*, SCM Press 1986

Michael Fogarty, *The Just Wage*, Chapman 1961

Peter Golding and Sue Middleton, *Images of Welfare: Press and Public Attitudes to Poverty*, Martin Robertson 1982

Michael Ignatieff, *The Needs of Strangers*, Chatto and Windus 1984

Luke T. Johnson, *Sharing Possessions*, SCM Press 1986

Keith Joseph and Jonathan Sumption, *Equality*, John Murray 1979

Michael Keeting and James Mitchell, *Easterhouse – An Urban Crisis*, Strathclyde Papers on Politics 47, Strathclyde University Politics Department, Glasgow 1986

Julian Le Grand, *The Strategy of Equality*, Allen and Unwin 1982

Alastair MacIntyre, *After Virtue*, Duckworth 1982

Joanna Mack and Stewart Lansley, *Poor Britain*, Allen and Unwin 1985

T.H. Marshall *Citizenship and Social Class*, Cambridge University Press 1950

José P. Miranda, *Marx and the Bible – A Critique of the Philosophy of Oppression*, SCM Press 1977

William D. Morris, *The Christian Origins of Social Revolt*, Allen and Unwin 1949

Redmond Mullin, *The Wealth of Christians*, Paternoster Press 1983

Scottish Council for Community and Voluntary Organisations, *Poverty in Scotland*, Briefing Paper No. 1, SCCVO, Edinburgh 1986

David Sheppard, *Bias to the Poor*, Hodder and Stoughton 1983

A. Sinclair, *Sewing It Up: Coates Paton's International Practices*, SEAD, Edinburgh 1982

Ruth L. Sivard, *World Military and Social Expenditures 1986*, World Priorities, Washington, DC 1986

R. Smail, *Breadline Scotland*, Low Pay Pamphlet 43, Low Pay Unit, London 1986

D.M. Smith, *Where the Grass is Greener*, Penguin 1979

R.H. Tawney, *The Acquisitive Society*, Bell and Son 1921

Peter Townsend, *Poverty in the United Kingdom*, Penguin 1979

US Roman Catholic Bishops' Pastoral Letter, 'Economic Justice

for All: Catholic Social Teaching and the US Economy',
Origins, NC Documentary Series, Vol. 16, No. 24, 1986

Ed. Alan Walker, *The Poverty of Taxation – Reforming the Social
Security and the Tax Systems*, Poverty Pamphlet 56, Child
Poverty Action Group, London 1982.

Tony Walter, *All You Love is Need*, SPCK 1985a

Tony Walter, *Fair Shares? An Ethical Guide to Tax and Social
Security*, Handsel Press 1985b

Michael Walzer, *Spheres of Justice*, Blackwell 1983

FURTHER READING

Archbishop of Canterbury's Commission on Urban Priority Areas, *Faith in the City – A Call for Action by Church and Nation*, Church House Publishing 1985

Charles Avila, *Ownership: Early Christian Teaching*, Sheed and Ward 1983

Gordon Brown and Robin Cook, eds, *Scotland – The Real Divide: Poverty and Deprivation in Scotland*, Mainstream 1983

Church of England Board for Social Responsibility, *Not Just for the Poor: Christian Perspectives on the Welfare State*, Church House Publishing 1987

Charles Elliott, *Comfortable Compassion? Poverty, Power and the Church*, Hodder and Stoughton 1987

Duncan Forrester, *Christianity and the Future of Welfare*, Epworth Press 1985

John Harvey, *Bridging the Gap – Has the Church Failed the Poor?*, St Andrew Press 1987

Michael Ignatieff, *The Needs of Strangers*, Chatto and Windus 1984

Luke T. Johnson, *Sharing Possessions*, SCM Press 1986

Joanna Mack and Stewart Lansley, *Poor Britain*, Allen and Unwin 1985.

Redmond Mullin, *The Wealth of Christians*, Paternoster Press 1983

Report of the Independent Commission on International Development Issues, *North–South: A Programme for Survival*, Pan Books 1980

David Sheppard, *Bias to the Poor*, Hodder and Stoughton 1983

Peter Townsend, Charles Elliott and others, *Poverty Today*,

Occasional Paper Number 7, Centre for Theology and Public Issues, New College, Edinburgh 1986

Peter Townsend, *Poverty in the United Kingdom*, Penguin 1979

US Catholic Bishops' Pastoral Letter, *Economic Justice for All*, 1986

Alan Walker and Carol Walker, eds,*The Growing Divide: A Social Audit 1979–1987*, Child Poverty Action Group, London 1987

Tony Walter, *Fair Shares? An Ethical Guide to Tax and Social Security*, Handsel Press 1985.

INDEX